VICTOR TWO

VICTOR TWO

PETER 'YORKY' CROSSLAND

BLOOMSBURY

To Matthew and Damien, for the
undying love and support they have
given me through all the hard times

First published in Great Britain 1996
Bloomsbury Publishing Plc, 38 Soho Square, London W1V 5DF

Copyright © 1996 by Peter Crossland

The moral right of the author has been asserted

A CIP catalogue record for this book is available from the British Library

ISBN 0 7475 3031 9 (hbk)
ISBN 0 7475 3275 3 (pbk)

10 9 8 7 6 5 4 3 2 1

Typeset by Hewer Text Composition Services, Edinburgh
Printed in Great Britain by Clays Ltd, St Ives plc

CONTENTS

ACKNOWLEDGEMENTS

S ince this will probably be the only book I shall ever write, I would like to express my sincere thanks to a number of people. Nana and Aunt Barbara for taking on the difficult role of mother. My sisters Christine and Barbara for always being there, especially recently. Uncle Peter for giving me the inspiration to join the army in the first place. Also other family members: Uncle Brian, Aunt Mary, Uncle John, Aunt Betty and my brother-in-law John.

I must also thank my friends in the SAS and the Royal Green Jackets, both those still serving and ex-members. There are many of them and they know who they are.

Those men in our half-squadron group who are honest with themselves will bear out the content of this book: while their individual perception of events will doubtless be different, my overall view is a truthful one. Pete was without doubt the one who got us through the Gulf War. His cool, calm and professional manner on Victor Two was outstanding, and without his command and leadership men would certainly have been killed.

My thanks go also to John Napier, Mac McFaddian, Dave Mason, Dave Smith, Billy Hughes, Phil Ibbotson, Macker,

VICTOR TWO

Andrew Shaw, Dennis Keen, Tony Spencer, Tucker, Linda Hofa, John Dukas, Steve Graham, Peter, Marion, Irene, Ian, Granny, Johnny, Franny, Goggs, Yvonne, Jimmy, Isabel and Stanley.

Yvonne has stood by me through perhaps the most difficult time of my life; when I thought I was losing it completely, she held me together. Finally I must thank my boys Matthew and Damien, whom I love unashamedly.

PROLOGUE

We had been in position since 0630 hrs, having had quite a difficult time finding a suitable place to lie up for the day. For once the weather was quite beautiful and, despite the nippy breeze, the sun shone in a clear blue sky. Apart from the odd spoon clanking against a mess tin, or the whisper of murmuring voices punctuated by a dirty laugh, the camp was in silence.

This serenity was suddenly broken by a rumbling noise – the distinctive sound of a vehicle getting closer. Most of us who were not asleep heard it. All around me swivelling heads popped up, searching to identify the threat. I looked over to my left, where Joey was in the sentry position. He had seen a vehicle heading directly towards our position and was frantically pointing over to our right. His balled fist with thumb pointing down could mean only one thing – enemy.

'Fucking hell,' I said to no one in particular. 'There's a fucking Iraqi vehicle coming towards us.'

For ten seconds it was headless chicken time. Guys grabbed weapons, tripping over each other in their attempts to get to a good firing position – you could almost taste the adrenaline.

This was what we were here for, to locate, close and kill the enemy, and it was about to happen.

Professionalism soon took over. Weapon in hand ready to acquire my target, I nestled down into a good firing position. Swiftly looking round, I could see Pat getting himself behind the machine gun on the Land Rover, while Ian, who was next to me, took up position under the camouflage net. Mel was crouched to my right, and Matt was just behind me. At times like this, firepower is what it's all about. With enough of it you can take on the devil.

Amid the rush to get into position, none of us had noticed that Mitch was still sound asleep in his green maggot. Since we were unable to risk waking him, he had to stay there until I had fired the first round. Mitch likes to think of himself as Mr Cool, so it was hilarious watching him jump out of his skin.

As the vehicle drew closer there was nothing but the sound of the engine. We knew our location was not what it should be, and we had moved in hurriedly. The Iraqis must have spotted us from some distance as they drove directly into the camp area and stopped within 20 metres of us. Luckily they must have thought that we were friendly forces, not thinking that enemy troops could be so close to Baghdad.

Matt whispered from behind, 'What the fuck are they doing?'

I ignored the question and watched the driver and front-seat passenger get out. The driver then walked to the front of his vehicle and opened up the bonnet.

'Matt. Yorky. Get ready. Cover me,' said Mel. 'I'm going out to meet him.' Mel was about to play the hero.

Breaking cover, he walked out to meet them. It was incredible to see the enemy so close. The officer was a short, slightly chubby guy in his early to mid-thirties, tidy and clean-shaven. He had dark hair and the very small moustache favoured by Middle Eastern men.

PROLOGUE

Mel emerged from under the camouflage net, his weapon held to his side to prevent it being seen.

The Iraqi approached, a look of bewilderment on his face. His head-dress, a blue beret, had the Iraqi eagle emblem badge on it, and he was wearing the insignia of a captain. We discovered later that his authority was that of a lieutenant colonel or even higher. What we didn't know was that the vehicle, a Russian Gaz 69, had more Iraqi troops in the back. The officer, complete with map-case and charts, continued to walk towards Mel. Not until he was three metres away did he realise we were the enemy.

Mel swung his rifle up and fired. Nothing happened. Automatically he dropped to his knees to clear the weapon stoppage, and by doing so he cleared my line of sight to the Iraqi. I fired and the man fell dead.

With that the world erupted as everyone else opened fire. Lights like starshells exploded in my brain as the rounds spat and cracked like a bushfire consuming dried-out vegetation. I saw the driver's body do a little death dance before it finally crumpled to the ground. In a rush we all broke cover together, heading towards the vehicle. It never dawned on me at the time, but we had just initiated the first contact of the ground war and the first kill of Operation Desert Storm was down to me. It was also the first time I had ever killed a man.

1

TOUGH BEGINNINGS

K illing is a serious business. I should know, because it is what I do for a living – or did until recently. I have often wondered about the effect of the sudden and violent extinguishing of life on the rest of us, and on the universe in general. We kill animals bred for food; we also hunt and kill rats, rabbits and other creatures classed as vermin – and we do it without thinking. The serious part starts when man kills his fellow men. Sometimes we can square our conscience here too: Jews, Palestinians, and, of late, Iraqis have all been regarded in certain quarters as the human equivalent of vermin.

It is claimed that over a hundred thousand Iraqi soldiers died in the Gulf War. Many died, and were buried at the same time, during the relentless bombing of their trenches by the Coalition air forces. Many others met their end in the retreat from Kuwait city, as tanks and military trucks intermingled with civilian vehicles. But when the Coalition war machine found them, hell swiftly followed: not the end of a useful life; not the comfort of an aged death surrounded by family members; but the burning flesh, insane screaming and white-hot metal delivered by modern weaponry. We of the Coalition rejoiced, having mentally dehumanised these young Iraqi soldiers. To us that long convoy winding along the road to Basra, staggering under the weight of loot extracted from Kuwaiti citizens, was just a single poisonous snake which we had beheaded with smart bombs, fired from an untouchable distance. But what we had really killed were students, peasant farmers, husbands and fathers. They were men who would be mourned by those left behind, men who had been loved, men who had lived their lives with dignity, men who had now inhaled the burning air and felt the pain of seared flesh.

Five years on, and the memory is still there. Whether rightly or wrongly, we should not kill without feeling guilt. As I watch my own dying son suffer, perhaps those hundred thousand voices are echoing through the universe and blaming me, for I am not without guilt.

I killed the first Iraqi of the ground war during the Gulf conflict. This book tells my remarkable story, and the truth about what really happened to an SAS fighting patrol deep behind the lines. Just getting into Iraq proved to be more of a comedy than a military operation. Then we were instructed to search out Scud missiles. It was a vital mission, for it was the only way the Americans could persuade the Israelis to stay out of the conflict and save the delicate balance of the Coalition.

As the Scud threat lessened, new orders were received, this time to assault the Iraqi microwave station known as Victor Two. It was a daring raid, claimed to be the largest single action undertaken by special forces inside Iraq. One half-squadron of SAS men were committed to the operation, which required both daring and stealth. Despite the staged attack that we had carefully planned, when the time came we just drove our heavily armed fighting column straight into the position. After placing the explosive charges under the very noses of the Iraqis we made to leave. Then all hell broke loose. In the ensuing fire-fight we took on odds of thirty to one before eventually breaking out. With the explosive charges echoing in our rear, the whole column disappeared into the darkness once more.

You might think we should have come home as heroes, but, as with all SAS operations, anonymity followed. And my personal life was never to be the same again. I returned to a broken marriage and a dying son. I am far from perfect, and I admit I have been unfaithful; still, I love my two boys and I loved my job. But trying to hold together both my professional and personal life created unbearable pressures. My son Matthew has muscular dystrophy, and his health is steadily declining. Now, at eighteen, it is just a matter of time. Eventually I looked for happiness in a second marriage, but that too ended in disaster. The SAS was indifferent and did little to help.

So in the dark hours when most of you are asleep, I lie awake and the tears roll down my cheeks. When I do sleep, I have nightmares. Matthew's face replaces that of a dead Iraqi soldier, as if my own violent actions are somehow responsible for his illness. Then with the dawn I have to face the world once more. So this is not just the story of another SAS soldier – it is about a man who has been to the very edge of life, and who for the past five years has faltered on the brink. I cannot step back, not until the day Matthew dies.

My name is Peter, but everyone calls me Yorky. I got the name not because I eat a lot of chocolate, but because I come from Yorkshire. I was born in Leeds in 1961. Three days after my birth my mother developed thrombosis, and it was several weeks before she and I could go home to our family's modest two-up, one-down terraced house with its outside toilet. But after only three days she suffered a heart attack and was rushed back to hospital. One week later, on Friday, 29 November 1961, Mum died. She was just twenty-nine.

At this terrible time for everyone the question of what was to happen to my two sisters, then two and four, and their new baby brother had to be resolved. At first it was suggested that I should be adopted: my Uncle Terry and Aunt Barbara, and the matron of the maternity hospital where I had been looked after while Mum was being treated for her thrombosis, both offered to take me. Dad was uncertain: he wanted to keep the family together if at all possible. In the end it was Nana, my maternal grandmother, who settled the matter. She and Aunt Barbara between them would bring up us children.

Nana was at that time fifty-six years old. She had brought up her own family while working full-time in a textile mill, and was still working when she made the decision to retire and raise this second family. But as Nana used to remind me as I grew up, we were the children of her daughter Kathleen, and she loved us.

Being just a few weeks old, I was of course totally oblivious to all these happenings. But I do remember Nana saying years later that it had been an incredibly difficult time for everyone. My two sisters continually nagged her with questions. Why had Mum gone away? When was she coming home? Both Nana and Dad told the girls that Mum had gone to heaven to see Jesus, and would be looking over them to make sure they were always safe. When I was older I learnt that my mother had foreseen her own death, and had written a letter to my elder sister, Christine, explaining that she had to go away and telling her to look after her young sister and new baby brother. I began to draw strength from her memory. Mum, knowing that she was dying, must have called on every ounce of courage she had. Her courage became my courage and today I need it more than ever.

Although we no longer lived under the same roof I saw quite a lot of my Dad as I grew up. Then, just before I left school, he became ill. One Monday evening in December 1975 he failed to go to work, which was unheard of. Dad had worked behind the bar at the local working men's social club for years – it was his second job, which brought in some much-needed extra money.

As a young man he had played Rugby League, and had even signed to go semi-professional for Keighley. That had all ended when he had shattered his ankle, but he had kept his fitness up. After Mum's death he had, however, taken to drinking more than was good for him, and he always smoked fifty cigarettes a day. But I had never known Dad feel ill before, and to see him in this condition now frightened me.

The doctor came, said there was nothing to worry about, and wrote out a prescription for some pills. The nearest chemist was some three miles away; I ran fast all the way, thinking that the sooner I got back the sooner Dad would get better. But the pills had no effect. After Christmas Dad got worse, and in January 1976 he went into hospital where he was kept heavily sedated. I was only fourteen and didn't really understand what was going on.

As Dad's condition deteriorated he started doing things which were totally out of character. One day, while most of his family were visiting, a young nurse came over to the bed. Out of the blue, Dad stuffed his hand straight up her skirt. The female members of the family tried to hide their embarrassment, while the men just burst out laughing. Later on, Nana told me that the drugs he was taking had made him delirious.

One afternoon while I was sitting with him he turned to me and said, 'Son, son.'

'Yes, Dad. I'm here.'

'I love you, son.'

I felt slightly embarrassed. I loved him, but the words had not been spoken since I was a baby.

'I love you too, Dad,' I replied, wishing I had said so more often. Today both my own lads still tell me they love me, as I regularly do to them.

The following day was a Saturday, so I didn't visit Dad because I was playing football. I told him that I would go and see him the following morning. At twelve minutes past six on Sunday morning I suddenly awoke from a deep sleep. About nine o'clock my sister Christine turned up at the house and told Nan and me that Dad had gone. He had died of cirrhosis of the liver and cardiac failure at the exact moment when I had woken up.

Nana and the rest of the family said many things about Dad and his health; from what I can deduce he had not been the same since Mum's death. I cannot recall a single occasion on which I saw him with another woman; instead, he had found his solace in the bottle. At least Mum and Dad are together again now.

I left school at fifteen and got my first job working as a warehouse boy for a cash and carry firm, unloading trucks and pricing products before taking them into the shop where I would stack the shelves. The only thing I can say in its favour is that it paid a wage. The day started at 8.30 and finished at five o'clock, but I could increase my pay by working overtime.

During this time I struck up a relationship with a local girl. Her name was June and I had known her for years as she lived in a flat opposite Nana's house. She was two years older than me, and a real looker. Around this time I started to realise that women found me attractive. I was quite big for my age, and with all the work in the warehouse I had become very fit and well-muscled. And I was just at the age when my sex drive was beginning to run riot. I spent most of the day dreaming about the things I could do with June, and most of the night doing them. We were both young and foolish, and she got pregnant. Nana was not amused, but the deed was done and that was that.

Matthew was born when I was sixteen years old, by which time I had moved in with June to share her small flat. When I took her to the hospital, once the nurses on duty had admitted her they told me to go home, thinking that I was June's younger brother rather than her boyfriend. I was totally ignorant about my rights and just did as I was told!

June had originally decided to put the baby up for adoption, but that was before Matthew was born. When we talked about it afterwards we both agreed that we would stop the adoption process: seeing our own child made us realise that there was no way we were going to part with him. It was then that we decided to call him Matthew, after the name in the bible; in truth it was also the title of a John Denver song that I particularly liked.

With hindsight, this was one of the best decisions I have ever made. At that time we had no idea that Matthew was ill. It was not until he was four and a half years old, and June and I were living in Germany, that we discovered something was wrong. I was so pleased about being a father that I just concentrated on being a responsible parent. I stuck the job in the warehouse for twelve months, then got the sack for bad time-keeping. Bollocks to them – I wanted to join the army anyway!

I had originally wanted to join the Parachute Regiment, but my Uncle Peter talked me out of it. He had started off in the REME, the Royal Electrical and Mechanical Engineers, before progressing into the newly formed 22 Special Air Service during the Malayan emergency in the 1950s. I took his advice, which as it turned out was good. In the end I opted for the Royal Green Jackets, and was sent for basic training at Peninsular Barracks in Winchester on 13 October 1978. I completed my training, but because I was under eighteen I was too young to join the Battalion. So I stayed at the training depot until I joined the 3rd Battalion, the Royal Green Jackets, stationed just outside Cambridge. Then life became really interesting.

Over the years I have been extremely promiscuous, in particular when I was with my first wife. I was like a dog on heat, never bothering about who I might be hurting. In the early part of my military career June stayed in Yorkshire with the children, while I lived in the army camp. This was a God-given opportunity to act like a single man, with the added perk of going home at weekends whenever I felt like it.

Like so many towns with a large local military presence, Cambridge had a 'groupie' element. Squaddies use certain pubs or clubs in which you will always find plenty of girls looking for a good time. We would all catch the bus that left from the camp guardroom at 1800 hrs every night. The last bus would return at 2230 hrs, but normally it was empty. If you managed to score with a bird, you either found a place to shag her up against the wall or you got her into camp. The latter was the real challenge – it was living proof to your mates that you could get the women.

It was also a challenge to beat the service system, mainly the regimental police. To sneak a girl into barracks we would get off at the previous bus stop and walk in through a side gate near the football pitches. There was an old RAF camp with no perimeter fence that bordered our barracks, and we could slip through. At that time the Northern Ireland threat was not very great and security was very relaxed. So you could literally walk in with your woman, fuck her all night, then kick her out the next morning. This seems a little tough on the women, but they enjoyed the experience as much as the guys and were always eager to participate. In the morning they would just walk down to the phone box and call a taxi.

At one time, the commanding officer and the RSM tried stopping this practice by getting the provost sergeant and his staff to mount operations against us. But this only increased the element of challenge, and some of us went to extraordinary lengths to get women into camp. Me and my mate Matt, who had a big Volvo, picked up two birds in a pub one night. They were desperate to come back to camp with us, but we explained that the only way we could get them in would be in the boot of the car. Somewhat reluctantly, they agreed to arrive in this manner. We casually drove into camp past the guardroom and parked outside our accommodation block. Seconds later we were all out of the car and in our bedrooms. Some hours later, feeling pretty pleased with ourselves, we reversed the process and got the girls out. We thought we had been really clever.

Then we heard about one of the lads from B Company. He had brought a girl into camp, and next morning she was still there. He decked her out in full camouflage clothing together with a regimental beret, the idea being that she could simply walk past the main gate and not be stopped. But as she approached the gate she walked across the grass of the nearby football pitch, which, unbeknown to her, was out of bounds. Suddenly, a loud voice rang out in her direction.

'You, soldier! What the fuck are you doing walking on my grass? Come here, you little piece of dog shit.' It was big Georgie Brown, the largest, meanest provost sergeant that ever lived. The young girl kept walking, looking straight ahead, praying that his words were directed at someone else.

As her pace quickened, the voice rang out for a second time. 'You, boy, stand still!'

She broke from a trot to an erratic jog. By this time Georgie was obviously ready to explode. He shouted to the sentries at the gate, who had witnessed the whole bizarre affair in total disbelief.

'Go fucking get him! I want him in my fucking guardroom!'

The two sentries ran to intercept the little figure, and, one on either side, she was marched into the guardroom, head held low.

'What's your fucking name and number?' Georgie bellowed, hooking the regimental beret off with his finger. The girl's hair fell to her shoulders. Georgie stepped closer in amazement. 'Nice pair of high-heeled shoes, my dear. How long have you been a member of the Royal Green Jackets, then?'

The young girl immediately broke into tears, swiftly informing on the soldier who had so callously got her into trouble. Georgie, big and ugly as he might have seemed, was himself a family man with a daughter of the same age.

'OK, my dear, let's get you sorted out. How about I make us a nice cup of tea, then get you a taxi home?'

The girl stopped sobbing and Georgie whispered to the two sentries, 'Go get that little fucking toe-rag now.' Ten minutes later the soldier was marking time in one of the prison cells, where he stayed for the next twelve days. The young girl put on her own clothes, drank her tea, then disappeared in a taxi paid for by Georgie – the biggest, meanest, but most humane provost sergeant you ever did see.

Amid all this infidelity, I still found the energy to go home to Leeds and perform with June. One weekend, just before the battalion were due to go to Northern Ireland, I received a phone call from June who informed me that she was pregnant again. I was twenty years old when Damien was born, and living like a single man. I thought it was time to grow up.

The Royal Green Jackets were posted to South Armagh in May 1981. Gone were the girls; it was time for some serious soldiering. We were housed in Bessbrooke Mill, a rambling old building which had once been a factory and which has been converted to accommodate a whole army regiment. Soldiers sleep, shit and shower all under the same roof. The only time you go out is when you are patrolling. Then you leave either by vehicle, or more likely by helicopter. You go out on operation, come back, report, eat, sleep, watch a video and repeat the whole process over and over. This may sound monotonous, but I loved it. Working in South Armagh can be very exciting.

Raymond McCreish, a twenty-four-year-old IRA terrorist, was the third hunger striker to die for the cause. On the day they moved his coffin from Newry hospital, some twenty thousand supporters followed the procession to his house. According to tradition, the coffin was taken inside to be the focus of a period of mourning. Three days earlier, my platoon had set up an observation point in woodland on the side of Camalough mountain.

At first light we were dropped off a couple of kilometres to the south by Wessex helicopter. We then moved off into the forest and located a vantage point that would give us cover yet also provide a bird's eye view of Camalough village, especially the cemetery which was our main target area. There were three patrols of four men; two would cover the flanks and rear, while I was to be the corporal in charge of the group watching the graveyard. Sitting around in an OP for several days can be very cold, so we had packed plenty of rations and extra warm clothing.

We set up our OP on the edge of a large block of woodland. Our task was primarily intelligence-gathering, so we were armed with SLRs (self-loading rifles), GPMGs (general-purpose machine guns) and M79 grenade launchers, plus personal radios and other specialist gear. Additionally we carried optical equipment for observing long distances by both day and night – the standard binoculars and a self-focusing Swiss scope, which are very basic compared to what the SAS would have used in the same situation. Although we had a camera and would try to photograph any IRA players in the procession, it was going to be impossible at a distance of two kilometres. Once again, the SAS with their hi-tech photographic equipment would have been able to take clear facial shots even from that distance. We, on the other hand, would have to crawl forwards when the time came and get as close as possible to the crowd. This is called a close target recce or CTR, and it was definitely going to be one of the highlights of the operation – especially if we were seen.

For the first couple of days there was very little activity to report, but on the Friday it all started. The population of the village increased dramatically until there were people everywhere, filling the streets and popping in and out of each other's houses. I reported to the battalion headquarters, who decided they would like some photographs of people in the crowd. As we were dressed in military uniforms and our faces were covered in camouflage cream, I decided the best thing to do was to brass-neck it down the hill. Three of us went – myself, Spud, the photographer, and Mitch, who was acting as cover man. It was common sense really, because the army patrolled this way all the time and three soldiers in a field would not arouse much attention.

We moved down the hill, and then walked across fields amongst the sheep and cows just like a farmer would do. Within one hundred metres of the procession, and still without anyone taking any serious notice of us, Spud took about five spools of film. Then, not wanting to push our luck, we turned round and walked steadily back up the hill. Just in case anyone was watching us, we entered the woods well short of the OP and then moved around in a pre-arranged deceptive plan. These tactics worked. We were not followed, and the OP was not compromised.

As the procession circled the village, young men could be seen pointing sticks into the hedgerows, and in some cases even setting them on fire, especially around the cemetery. This is standard IRA procedure for dealing with any close SAS OPs, and the farmers had in fact cut some of the hedges so low that all the foliage had disappeared. Despite these precautions the SAS, I was to discover later, could get a patrol in anywhere should the need arise. Whatever, on this day none of the youths seemed bothered about walking two kilometres up the side of the mountain to check out the woods.

As the afternoon wore on I observed activity in the cemetery, which was just 50 metres from McCreish's house, particularly around the newly dug grave. Two men produced a package about the size of a biscuit tin wrapped in a black bag and placed it in the hedgerow opposite the grave. From then on, one of them stood by it all the time. This seemed odd and I reported it at once to our commanding officer, Major Pringle. Two minutes later he came back on the radio, very excited. We all knew the package most probably contained the pistols for the firing party – a typical act of defiance by the IRA on such occasions. However, the guards never left the package and they were changed over every hour or so. As night fell Major Pringle decided to bring us back to the Mill, where I could fully brief him and the platoon commander. Then I would take the platoon commander back to the OP, and carry out a CTR on the package and the surrounding area.

When we returned, the village had become much quieter. The only noises were coming from McCreish's house, where a wake was well in progress. It was a perfect night for the CTR – clear, with no moon – which would allow us to get very close to the target area. The CTR group consisted of the platoon commander, Mitch, Freddie and me. We moved fairly quickly, getting as close to the graveyard as possible. As we neared the hedgerow that surrounded it, we could see in front of us and slightly to our right the hole that had been dug for the coffin. McCreish's house, where the mourners were still hard at it, was just across the road. Having first removed our webbing, and leaving Mitch to cover our backs, we moved off, crawling silently on our bellies towards the grave and the hidden package.

Suddenly the guard turned round – he might have heard us or seen our silhouette. 'Who's that?' The voice was sharp and sounded scared.

'Fucking hell, we've been seen!' I whispered to no one in particular. At the same time I could hear my heartbeat go up two notches. We were just about to jump up when another voice rang out.

'It's only me, Michael!' An Irish accent – the guard was about to be relieved of his duty. The sense of relief at not being discovered was overwhelming. Unfortunately, they both sat down on the bank by the package and started chatting. It had taken us over an hour to get into this position, just six metres from the package, and time was getting short. It was frustrating, but I made the decision to lift off in the hope that our time would come tomorrow. We crawled away, and once we were out of hearing range made our way back to the pick-up point.

The helicopter arrived and we were once more extracted back to Bessbrooke Mill.

Next morning, the guys were all ready to go again. We had decided to move back into the same OP, using roughly the same route that we had taken the previous night. There was some danger of ambush, and we would have to be more cautious. The rest of the team – those who had not been with us the previous evening – had been briefed an hour earlier. Even though they knew the area, and we had been into the same OP, the operation still needed to be coordinated.

Three patrols, twelve men in total, formed up on the helipad. Flying south from Bessbrooke, we headed in the direction of Newry and Camalough mountain. On landing ten minutes later, all the guys jumped out quickly and the helicopter took off again immediately. There is always an eerie silence once a chopper has departed, as if you have been abandoned.

Patrolling with care, we made our way back to the block of woodland, hiding in the sanctuary of the trees. As we neared our old OP I called the guys together and gave them a quick recap of what was going to happen. Then, after checking to see if there had been any activity around the OP area, we moved back into our positions. While Mitch and I set up the optics and the radio equipment, the other guys erected camouflage nets to provide overhead cover. We were a little lower than the top of the mountain, and it was just possible that a farmer might discover us.

When we were settled, we spent the first hour observing the activity that was building up both in the cemetery area and around McCreish's house. Once again we noted the young men, or 'dickers' as they are known, start beating and prodding at the hedgerows and setting fire to the thicker ones. We quickly settled into our routine, reporting events as they happened directly back to the OC at the Mill.

By mid-morning the crowds had increased dramatically, and

by lunchtime more than twenty thousand were waiting for the funeral to start. About two o'clock the procession started to congregate around McCreish's house, waiting for the coffin to be brought out. The crowd looked anxious and worked up, and my best guess was that they were expecting some sort of firing party. But normally a salute of this kind would not be fired until they had paraded the coffin around the village.

Eventually the coffin came out, carried by a group of men wearing black balaclavas and the traditional black paramilitary uniform. The crowd stayed behind the funeral procession, but as it neared the cemetery people started massing on all sides. Overhead we could see one of our Puma helicopters observing the procession from about 2000 feet. At times it would drop lower, to about 1000 feet, giving the on-board high-powered heli-tele brilliant coverage. This device allows the operator to observe detailed targets such as faces with great clarity from up to two kilometres away. The IRA did not know much about this highly sensitive piece of equipment, nor did they fully understand what it could do. It was useful from our point of view, because it made them pay more attention to the helicopter than to any soldiers who might be lurking in the surrounding countryside.

As the activity started mounting, so did our excitement. The reporting went in stages: informing on the build-up of the cortege, where the people were, and who was doing what. In particular we tried to monitor and identify members of Sinn Fein and any known IRA sympathisers. A solid block of people, all male, formed a loose line giving unrestricted access from the house to the graveyard. There was also a lot of activity in various households. On such occasions everybody in the village leaves their doors open. If anything happens during a funeral, the firing party can then escape to any house within the village, dropping their weapons as they run.

17

Just before the operation was mounted that morning, my final briefing from the OC informed me that my reporting had to be absolutely on the ball. Not only were the whole battalion of the Royal Green Jackets listening in, but my reports were being fed directly to the Ministry of Defence in Whitehall, who were monitoring the situation. Events such as hunger strikes swayed public opinion not just in Great Britain but around the world. But it never influenced our operation reporting – we just reported things as we saw them.

As the cortege started its final journey into the cemetery, one of the guys in the OP indicated some movement just to our left. I looked towards the side of the hill and saw a man standing about a hundred metres away. It was quite obvious that he was just a farmer checking his sheep, but the problem was that he had a dog with him – and a dog can easily give away the position of an OP. As the farmer moved towards us, my heart started pumping adrenaline around my body. But we were well camouflaged, and if necessary we would hold him until the funeral was over. In the event, the farmer hung around for a couple more minutes and then started off down the hillside towards the village.

Although we had missed some five minutes of the cortege, one of the guys had been observing and writing everything down in a log. I was soon back in radio contact with the operations room at Bessbrooke Mill. There was a quick reaction force standing by there, and as the activity built up all the radio channels were switched to our frequency. Most of the guys back at Bessbrooke were waiting on the helipad ready to do a quick snatch if and when the need arose. In the past, the Marines had tried to do a snatch of both weapons and firing party at a hunger striker's funeral in Belfast. This had caused uproar and in Northern Ireland uproar can quickly turn into a riot. However, our OC had decided to keep his troops well out of the way but ready to mount an instant operation if required.

The aim of our own operation on the ground was not to worry about snatching the firing party, but to get the weapons.

When the procession came in line with the house, three men came out under cover of umbrellas. Umbrellas were often used to cover the movement of an IRA firing party, because it helped the gunmen avoid identification from a helicopter overhead. However, we were observing the action from a more oblique angle, and we could clearly see underneath the umbrellas. This enabled us to report that three men were coming out of McCreish's home carrying what looked like rifles. They ran towards the coffin and quickly lined up next to the grave. The umbrellas came down, and the firing party presented two volleys of three shots each. The instant they had finished the umbrellas came up, covering the firing party once more. It was a very professional operation. Equally efficiently they moved back into McCreish's house.

This is when the activity really started. From the house three figures appeared, carrying long objects in black bin liners. It was impossible at this stage to identify the shapes as rifles, but the odds were very good that this is what they were. The figures moved from the house into the back garden, and from there into someone else's house. In this fashion they made their way steadily out of the village. Finally they emerged north of it, by the main road. They were now opposite a large field where thousands of people were congregating. We could now tell that they were three men no older than sixteen, all dressed in military parkas with the hoods up. Suddenly we saw them move into a thick, large hedgerow. Again because of our vantage point we could look down on them. At this stage I positively identified the butt of a weapon sticking out from a bin liner: it was either a .303 Lee Enfield or a Garand. The young men were in the hedgerow for no more than two minutes. When they reappeared, they were empty-handed. Walking to the field, they disappeared into the crowd.

19

It took about two hours for the huge crowds to disperse and the village to return to its normal quiet existence. After making a note of the eight-figure grid reference where the weapons had been hidden, we made radio contact with base and passed on the information. On this basis the OC decided to send one of the platoons into the area where they could positively identify the location of the weapons. From here they would pinpoint them with the assistance of a special weapons sniffer dog. Then the platoon would set up an ambush and wait for the IRA to collect the guns – a task normally undertaken by the IRA unit's quartermaster. To arrest him and take the weapons would constitute a successful operation. The ambush platoon waited all night, but no enemy showed. This was very disappointing, and I put it down to the somewhat clumsy way in which the platoon had entered the area.

The following morning they were extracted together with the weapons. We were picked up a little later by helicopter and flown back to Bessbrooke Mill. It was a job well done, and we got a round of congratulations from the OC and other members of the squadron. At 0500 hrs the next morning we went out with the rest of the company on a massive round-up of other known terrorists who had been present at the funeral. In all it was a very successful operation – something the battalion really needed, as it had not been a good tour of Northern Ireland. We had lost six men, all killed by the IRA. A further two were wounded, one severely – to this day he is still paralysed from where he was shot in the spine. We also lost an ammunitions technical officer blown up trying to dismantle a bomb outside Newry. I was awarded the GOC's commendation, which was a bit of a mockery considering the operation we had mounted. In the same list of citations, cooks and pay corps clerks received the same award for sitting behind a desk or frying chips. But I had enjoyed some real soldiering, and that was the most important thing.

In May 1982, the battalion was posted to Germany. This time June and the boys came with me, and I think that was the best part of our married life – until we discovered what was wrong with Matthew. Muscular dystrophy is a muscle-wasting disease which is carried by the female and passed on to the male. It is caused by a defective gene. I am no expert on the details of its origins, but I do know all too well what happens in practice. Matthew was four when he was diagnosed as having muscular dystrophy. It is a most horrific disease with totally devastating effects. One minute June was with the doctor thinking that maybe her child was a touch slow, or clumsy even. When he walked he took slightly wider steps than other children, lifting up on his toes and raising his knees higher than normal. She explained that sometimes his arms would pump back and forth as he used them to assist his balance – and yes, he did stumble. The army doctor calmly said, 'Your son has muscular dystrophy. He will be in a wheelchair by the time he is twelve, and he will not live beyond the age of eighteen.' That is exactly how a doctor at the British Military Hospital in Hanover informed June in 1983. She had taken Matthew alone, because I could not get off duty to go with her, but I met her off the bus as it pulled into the camp. Her face was twisted in agony, and I swear to this day she was temporarily deranged. The tears were running down her face. The other passengers on the bus had tried to console her, but she was unable to speak.

'What's wrong? What's the matter?' I was suddenly very frightened.

'No, no. I don't know.' She grabbed me, pulling at my sleeve, her words making no sense. The shock was so great that at first she could not tell me what was wrong. Even when I calmed her down she could not remember the name of the disease. She looked at Matthew and then at me, explaining what the doctor had said as she had understood it.

'He's going to die,' she stammered.

21

Now I knew why June looked insane, and the madness was contagious. That bastard army doctor had not even got a nurse to sit with her afterwards, had not bothered to inform the padre or even to get a message to me. To this day I cannot explain how I felt at that moment. I looked at my son, and he seemed fine. They must be wrong, I thought. Then I started to notice little things that were not right. The instinct is to wrap up the child immediately in cotton wool, but he doesn't know what's wrong. He still wants to be out there playing with the other kids. Matthew would try running and climbing with the others, but could never keep up. He could not understand and got very frustrated with the other children, including his younger brother, Damien. Then some of them would take the mickey out of him, not wanting to play with him because he was different. Kids can be so cruel. As time goes on, the effect on the physical condition of a child with muscular dystrophy is slow to progress – but progress it does.

We left Germany six months later, returning for two years to Winchester where I had been posted as a training corporal. After this it was my intention to try for SAS selection. While we were in Winchester Matthew's condition started to progress and he suffered more frequent falls, which obviously caused minor injuries, cuts and bruises. He was eight years old when I joined the SAS and we finally moved to Hereford. Over the next three years he deteriorated at a steady rate, despite his having regular physiotherapy in an attempt to slow down the shrinkage of his tendons. As the tendons shrink, stability is reduced, resulting in more accidents. This continues until eventually a child with muscular dystrophy is almost glad to go into a wheelchair. I remember many times picking Matthew up from the special school he attended, where he also received physio, and he would be in absolute agony. The treatment involved literally straightening his legs – stretching his tendons like an elastic band. Additionally he wore a leg brace, which he was supposed to keep on all day until he went to bed. The resulting pain was terrible, but it was an effort to prolong his active life. At times he never stopped screaming for me to remove it: 'Dad! Dad! Please take it off – it's hurting.' Matthew is no whinger, but an extremely brave boy who over the years has gone through hell and back. One day I could bear his screams no more; his pleading with me to remove the terrible contraption ripped through my soul. I ran into his room and took the brace off. He would never wear that damned thing again.

Within a couple of weeks Matthew was confined to a wheelchair and would never walk again. It was a couple of years before he eventually got an electric wheelchair, most kindly donated by a local pub in Hereford, the Game Cock. Three years later when he required a replacement the SAS Regimental Association bought him a new one. By this time his physical condition had worsened to the point where he was developing extreme spinal curvature, which can eventually compress the lungs and in extreme cases the heart. His hand movement had almost totally gone, so he had to be helped to eat. When he wanted to go to the toilet he had to be placed on the commode and held in position. All dressing, bathing, washing, shaving, and so on had to be done for him.

If you can imagine looking after a baby that is eighteen years old and weighs twelve stone, then you're close. I take my hat off to everybody who is in the same position. My son is also constantly contracting pneumonia and pleurisy, and has lost almost 80 per cent of his vital lung capacity due to his muscular weakness. Matthew now requires constant care, which is and will remain always my first priority.

2

A NEW LIFE IN HEREFORD

G etting to Hereford is one thing, but staying there is another. The SAS selection course is very hard. If I can offer any advice to would-be SAS members, it would be not to get over-fit. Wait until you start selection, and use the course itself to bring you to your peak. And never swap food for sleep. Always eat as much as you can stuff into your body, because you will burn calories at the rate of 6000-plus per day. Finally, don't give up. When you feel utterly destroyed and think you can't go any further, just say to yourself, 'I *can* do it.'

I found myself improving every day, which was just as well when the time came for the endurance march. This is no ordinary test. You are allowed between twenty and twenty-two hours, depending on the weather, to complete a rugged route through the Brecon Beacons, while carrying 55 lb in a bergen on your back. I completed it in seventeen hours, which I thought was a bloody good effort.

For our jungle training we went to Brunei. Not having been in such conditions before, it was a bit of a shock to me. One of the old-hand instructors said, 'Living in the jungle can be easy or hard – it simply depends on your personal attitude to it.' My one big mistake was spilling insect repellent on my private parts.

The whole jungle is teeming with insect life, much of which will attempt to eat you alive. Early one morning, while it was still dark, I was sitting in my sleeping bag putting some repellent on my boots when some of it accidentally dropped on my groin. Two minutes later I started to get a stinging sensation which quickly turned to a fierce burning pain. In desperation I dropped my trousers and tried to wash the stuff off, but it was too late because much of it had already soaked into my skin.

My cries attracted others, all highly amused at me with my trousers round my ankles and splashing water on my balls. They were already half as large again as they normally were, and I had a half-inch black patch across my dick. One of our medics, who realised how dangerous this could be, offered to help. But by this stage there was little anyone could do and I just had to take the pain.

All that day during instruction I found it difficult to concentrate. Next morning, after a very restless night, I discovered that my testicles had swollen to the size of tennis balls. To make matters worse we had a jungle patrol that day. It was sheer agony, but I was determined not to fail the training. By day four the area in question looked like two black billiard balls oozing green pus. My predicament was a constant source of entertainment for the rest of the course, who would gather each morning to watch me wrap my balls in bandages. Still, as with selection, I refused to give up.

The SAS combat survival course is the last physically demanding phase of selection. It is part of the joint services combat survival course, which is attended by military personnel from all over the world. During the two weeks of training you receive instruction in the art of surviving, and some good advice on resistance to interrogation. In the final week you go on the run as a prisoner of war.

Before being set free every prisoner undergoes a series of strip searches − not just equipment and clothing, but a complete body cavity search. There are no prizes for guessing what happens next. But a couple of guys on the course were boasting in a loud and somewhat big-headed manner; after the examination they came out looking rather sheepish and humbled. I know, because I was one of them. It didn't help me much when I shouted to the medical sergeant, 'I'll have the one with the biggest fingers!' That's just what I got. Real heartless bastards, those medics – no sense of humour. You are not supposed to have any money, and guys invent all sorts of elaborate ways to hide some about their person. Many of the lads fold a £20 note as small as possible, then put it in a condom and swallow it. Normally it will pass through the system in about twenty-four hours. A good mate of mine tried this – unfortunately he didn't see it again until after the exercise was over.

While you are running, a military unit acts as the hunter force. Its members are trying to catch you as you move from checkpoint to checkpoint. This teaches you to evade capture. The run starts when you are dropped off in the middle of Wales wearing a World War II battledress uniform and boots which are either too big or too small. A tobacco tin houses your survival equipment – a small sharp blade, something to make fire, a condom to carry water in, fish hooks and line, and a number of other useful little items.

Providing the weather is not too bad, the survival side can be quite exciting – that is, until you get captured and face interrogation. The hunter force don't mess about when they capture you, and somehow I finished up with a broken rib. No matter: once captured you are subjected to the regulation thirty-six hours of resistance-to-interrogation training. Hood on, stood in the stress position, feet spread with hands against the wall for hours. With a broken rib it was no joke. While all this is happening, they play what they call 'white sound'. It buzzes at you all the time, and is designed to wear you down or make you crack up.

Every couple of hours or so, you get dragged off into an interrogation room. Here you are put in front of a trained interrogator – some prat who obviously gets off on watching SAS candidates strip naked. Then he asks you loads of stupid questions, like where you come from, and what is your unit. Say nothing, and you pass the course.

So it was that in December 1986 I passed into the ranks of 22 SAS. I shall always remember receiving my beige beret with its famous winged dagger. I was posted to A Squadron, mobility troop, and stayed with them for most of my SAS service. It was a great troop, where I made some good friends and had an altogether brilliant life. June and the boys moved into married quarters and everything seemed fine. As I settled into the troop I quickly realised how different the SAS were when compared with the rest of the army. Guys would suddenly disappear, returning months later with a fantastic suntan, but would never let on where they had been. In Hereford operations seem to come out of the blue: the team is selected, and off they go. One classic operation took part in Northern Ireland while I was still a green rookie.

In May 1987 intelligence had been received to indicate that a police station was to be attacked by a method used a year before in County Armagh. In April 1986 a mechanical digger had been packed with explosives and driven into the RUC station at The Birches, causing widespread damage. A report that another JCB had been stolen in East Tyrone was now causing alarm bells to ring. All efforts were made to locate the digger and identify the target. After intensive covert searching, the weapons and explosives were located. Subsequently, the digger too was located in a derelict building on a farm some 15 kilometres away. Surveillance provided more information, and eventually the target was identified as the RUC station at Loughall, which was only manned part-time. The date and time of the attack were eventually confirmed.

Two of the IRA activists involved were named as Patrick Kelly and Jim Lynagh, who commanded the East Tyrone active service unit. When masked men stole a blue Toyota van from Dungannon Jim Lynagh was spotted in the town, which suggested that the van was to be used in the Loughall attack. Not long afterwards, the OP set up at the farm reported that the JCB was being moved. At this stage the SAS, who had been reinforced from Hereford, took up their ambush positions, mostly in a row of small fir trees lining the fence on the opposite side of the road to the police station. Several heavily armed stops were also in position, covering all avenues of escape.

At a little past 7p.m. on Friday, 8 May, the Toyota van drove down the road past the police station; several people were seen to be inside. It returned soon afterwards from the direction of Portadown, this time followed by the JCB with three hooded IRA terrorists in the cab. Declan Arthurs was driving with Michael Gormley and Gerald O'Callaghan riding shotgun. The bucket was filled with explosive contained in an oil drum, and partly concealed with rubble. While the blue van charged past the station, the JCB slammed through the gate. One of the two riding shotgun ignited the bomb, and then all three made a run for it. Back at the van, several hooded men jumped clear and started to open fire in the direction of the RUC station. It was at this stage that the SAS ambush was activated.

The sudden hail of fire was terrifying, and all eight IRA men fell under its ferocity. At the height of the fire-fight the bomb exploded, taking with it half the RUC station and scattering debris everywhere. As the dust settled, the SAS closed in on the bodies. At that moment a white car entered the ambush area. Both occupants were dressed in blue boiler suits similar to those worn by the IRA men, and were taken to be other terrorists. It did not help their cause when, seeing the ambush in progress, they stopped and started to reverse. One of the SAS stops opened fire, killing one of the occupants and wounding the other. It later transpired that the dead motorist, Antony Hughes, had nothing to do with the IRA. Several other vehicles and pedestrians soon appeared on the scene, but by this time the situation was stabilised. For this quiet village it was an incredible sight: the RUC station half demolished; a mess of mangled yellow metal that was once a JCB; and numerous bodies littering the street.

Without doubt Loughall was one of the most successful operations ever mounted against the IRA, who were totally stunned by the loss of two complete active service cells. The Hughes family were compensated for their loss, and, with no public inquest, the matter was closed. The IRA, believing that there was a mole in their organisation, had a period of self-assessment but did not lick their wounds for long. Six months later, at a Remembrance Day ceremony in Enniskillen, a massive bomb was detonated which killed eleven people and injured more than sixty.

By 1988 I was on the anti-terrorist team and it was my turn. We trained and prepared for anti-terrorist exercises, and were also liable for call-out. Call-out can be with the team deployed in the UK, or anywhere in the world.

I was part of a team sent to Northern Ireland to reinforce the team that was already over there. If a large operation demanded it, or the number of operations mounted required extra man-power, reinforcements from the anti-terrorist team were normally sent over. They were flown by helicopter from Hereford to Aldergrove, taken straight to the operations room and briefed.

On this particular job, various intelligence sources had indicated that the Irish People's Liberation Organisation (IPLO) were about to attempt to murder a part-time UDR soldier. Their chosen method would be what the SAS term CQA (close quarter assassination) – they were going to drive up to his farmhouse and blow him away. In the past their *modus operandi* had been to sneak up to one of the windows under cover of darkness, define the target's silhouette or shadow through the curtains, and shoot him. As there were two UDR soldiers living in close proximity, both had to be protected. I was assigned to one of the teams providing close protection from inside the two houses. The option that I was on seemed to be favourite.

Orders were given that afternoon, after which we were given time to prepare our equipment and eat something. We were to stay for as long as required. The operation started when I and the rest of the ten-man team drove down to the target's farm that night in two plain vans.

The UDR soldier owned a large farm with a lot of land, which posed a major problem for us. Whenever he left his house to feed his cattle or attend to any other farm work, it meant that we could not go with him. We compromised by picking out vantage points around the farm from where we could best cover him for the majority of the time. We stressed that on no account should he change his habits, as the terrorists might have been observing the farm for some time. If they noticed anything unusual happening now, the operation might be compromised.

Remaining well hidden, yet being able to provide instant cover, was not easy. Still, we felt confident that if anyone turned up at the house with murder in mind we would be well able to deal with the situation.

We would aim to arrest the terrorists, but if necessary we would engage and kill them.

The operation was so covert that when we went into the house the only person who knew about our presence was the farmer himself – none of his family was aware of our presence. The family consisted of a brother, sister-in-law, and two adult sons who lived in a house up a lane next to the farm. Even the dog that was shut up for most of the day seemed to accept our presence without barking. To all intents and purposes, this sleepy little farmyard was as it had always been.

It was a good team, made up of NCOs and governed by two sergeants. I and five other members were ordered to move into the house, while the four others split into two teams; one was positioned immediately outside the door in a coal shed, with the other hiding in the barn adjacent to the farmhouse from where they had a full view of the farmyard and the main door. The five of us in the house were also split up. Two of us were downstairs and two upstairs, leaving the team leader to provide close protection for the UDR man. Deploying our forces in this way gave us immediate control of any situation and would enable us to act as required, since we had good 'eyes on' in all areas. At night we had a different system. Two guys went outside to form a night standing patrol at the bottom of the driveway, and give us early warning if anyone approached the building.

The farmhouse itself was a four-bedroom place with an extensive loft, two big rooms downstairs and quite a large kitchen. Yet the only heating was a coal fire in the main living room next to the kitchen. Since it was mid-February, the house was freezing. We were probably as cold inside as the four guys outside. At least the two in the barn had lots of hay bales to nestle down in.

The target whom we were protecting was a forty-two-year-old part-time soldier who had been with the UDR for several years. He used to work two or three hours for them each week, seeing this as his duty to his country. The sole reason for the IPLO selecting him was that he was an isolated, easy target. Unfortunately, that is the sad injustice of the way in which these terrorists operate: they haven't got the bottle to attack a real target. Despite the threat to his life, the farmer was in very high spirits. Even so, we kept reassuring him that if anybody came near, we would get them before they got him.

Nick and I were downstairs in a little utility room about four feet square, whose window looked out at the back and down the 30 yards or so of driveway. During the day our main job was to report anybody coming up the drive and approaching the farmhouse. While one of us was doing that, the other could eat, rest or give a little bit of close protection to the UDR man. During the day we were able to use the kitchen to make tea or cook food, and distribute it to our mates elsewhere on the farm. The poor guys who were outside were unable to eat or brew up during the day, so at night hot brews and food would be taken out to them and they could stuff their faces.

As time passed, intelligence gave us better information on who we were actually looking after. It also gave us time to become acquainted with Tom, as the soldier liked to be called. He was a nice guy, and kept us amused with stories of some of the nasty little incidents in which he had been involved over the years.

One afternoon, Tom's family turned up at the farmhouse. This caused us major concern, because we were still in the utility room with the door wide open. Luckily we had seen them coming up the driveway, so it was just a matter of getting hold of Tom and telling him not to let them come near our hiding-place. For the next hour or so we had to listen to them all yapping away, keeping our fingers crossed that Tom would be able to keep them away from our little room without giving the game away.

On day five things started to happen. The road that ran around the farm became busy and the intelligence information started to increase, indicating that the hit was on. Late that morning a couple of cars with three or four people in each started driving past at irregular intervals; it was always the same cars, and always with the same number of passengers in them. We noted that they paid particular attention to the farmhouse and farm buildings, slowing down to get a closer view. It looked as if the terrorists were carrying out a recon-naissance of the target area. Because of this activity, and the fact that we reported it on our personal radios within the farm, Tom started to pick up the vibes that something was about to happen and he became a little nervous.

Late in the afternoon we received another message from control, indicating that something was definitely going to happen that evening. Because of this the team leader decided to make a few changes. He decided that the two-man team in the barn should stay put, but told the two who had previously been in the shed to move across to the far side of the barn. The intention was to trap the terrorists should they come from the rear of the farm complex, heading towards the barn. As for the two of us inside the house, I was told to move upstairs and leave Nick downstairs in the utility room. I went into the front bedroom, taking up position near the window where I could overlook the front and see down the driveway. There was also one guy in the back bedroom, covering the rear. The remaining two men would be deployed at the bottom of the drive, as they had been for the past couple of nights.

As darkness fell, it was quite obvious that things were happening. The adrenaline started to flow, and the guys, although slightly anxious, were operating at 100 per cent. Tom, however, was a different kettle of fish. He was constantly coming up to either Nick or me and asking us what was happening. Our UDR man was starting to look very, very scared. All we could do was reassure him that he had nothing to worry about. We told him to go back to the kitchen, which he used as his living room, and stay there. We had placed a chair there right up against the wall so that he could watch television without being in direct line of sight from any window, and we had already made sure that the blinds and curtains were all drawn.

Although we had detected no movement, around mid-evening the dog started to bark and continued to do so until about nine o'clock. This was weird – it had never done so before. Whether it had heard something, or was simply anxious for its master, is hard to say. About 2130 hrs Daniel, who was upstairs at the back of the building, reported car lights approaching from the bottom of the road to the farm. As the car approached the junction, its lights were turned off and it pulled over. Because of the darkness Daniel couldn't see exactly what was happening, or whether anybody got out. Then the vehicle's lights came back on, and it drove off again. Clearly some sort of activity was going on, and we had possibly witnessed a drop-off by the terrorists. About five minutes later two figures appeared at the bottom of the drive about 40 yards away. Nick, who had also spotted them, immediately sent a report to control: 'Standby. Standby. That's a definite. Two unknown X-rays at the bottom of the drive. Now static.' X-ray was the code name for a terrorist.

Control acknowledged, repeating exactly what Nick had said in order to confirm and to avoid any mistakes being made during the transmission. Nick continued: 'One unknown X-ray moving towards my location.' Again control repeated his message. As the 'unknown X-ray' got halfway up the drive, the farm's porch light came on and showed that he was carrying a weapon. Nick immediately transmitted: 'Standby. Standby. The unknown X-ray is definitely carrying a weapon. Looks like a possible shotgun.' This put everyone in a high state of alert: at that moment we all knew that the hit was about to take place. It was also obvious that this terrorist was going to move directly below the window, right underneath my position. The moment he was in my sights, I would be able to engage him if necessary.

As the terrorist started coming towards the window Nick continued his commentary. The man turned left and looked into the kitchen window behind which Tom was nervously watching television. The terrorist was most likely looking for shadows or silhouettes. If he had seen any, he would probably have fired through the window. Then at last I got the chance to see him. He was wearing a green or olive drab jacket of the type used by the British army several years ago, together with blue coveralls and black boots. A black balaclava covered his head and hid his face, and he was carrying a sawn-off shotgun. The report had indicated that these guys would probably turn up with compact, automatic shotguns, but this definitely was not the case.

Nick continued: 'Unknown X-ray now looking in my position.' The terrorist had stopped to look through the window of the utility room where he was sitting. Nick was pointing his weapon and also providing the commentary, which took quite a lot of nerve. In our briefing, the team leader had indicated that we were not to open fire unless we or Tom were positively under threat. At this stage Nick perceived that he was not under threat. I perceived the same, but we still aimed our weapons at the terrorist. The man then turned right and started to walk round the outside of the building.

Crack, crack, crack. Three shots rang out in rapid succession, and I ran quickly downstairs. A further four rounds were fired. Not knowing exactly where the firing was coming from, or who had done it, I thought it unwise to burst through the front door. Instead I moved to the back of the house and waited for Daniel to come downstairs. The moment he joined up with me we both jumped through the back door, moved round to the left side of the building and there met up with Matt.

We soon found the X-ray who had been hit. He was making no sound, but his body was still moving – although most of that twitching was the result of shock. He had been hit a number of times in the body and head and when I got a little closer I could see the terrible damage that the hits had inflicted on his body. I knew he was there to kill another man, and we had prevented an assassination attempt; nevertheless, bright red blood streaming on to the ground is not a pretty sight in any circumstances.

We quickly started scanning the area with our night sights,

trying to locate the second man. The incredible thing was that, although the terrorists had stood at the bottom of the drive, for some unknown reason our two-man unit there never saw them. They heard the running commentary, but never saw or identified any terrorists. An immediate search of the area eventually produced the terrorist's likely escape route. Our efforts to find him that night failed, but he was captured a couple of months later.

Whilst we were searching along the road, a car drove up. We stopped it, and discovered its driver to be Tom's sister-in-law. She was in a frantic state, thinking that her brother had just been killed. We calmed her down and said, 'You're okay. Tom's okay, too. Somebody's just tried to kill him, but he's safe. No problems at all.' The relief on her face was fantastic. A job well done.

We returned to Hereford and continued training, and thoughts of the dead man soon slipped from my mind. The main reason was Tara. Members of the anti-terrorist team stay around the camp most of the time, which led me to meet and fall in love with one of the WRACs stationed at Hereford. Tara was PA to the master chef. We met in the Paladrine Club, a social club on the camp, while both of us were on duty during a regimental reunion. We were together for most of the evening, got to chatting, and one thing soon led to another.

Looking back, it all began as a one-night stand. But pretty soon I was spending more time in the female block visiting Tara's room than I was going home. One day things came to a head, and June threw me out. What the hell – I think it was what I wanted. I moved back into barracks, as I had my own room there anyway. Not that I spent much time in it, because really I moved in with Tara.

The regiment makes no hard-and-fast rules about your personal life, providing it does not affect your work. The moment it does, you can kiss the SAS goodbye. The trouble started when June approached the married families officer and complained about my behaviour. I was on the carpet, and the message was clear: sort your personal life out and quick. My one saving grace was our troop sergeant, Robbo. He covered for me and warned me every time the shit was about to fly in my direction – much of it thrown by June.

Just about that time, while I was still on the team, another job came up. Robbo was to be in charge, and he selected his own team. I think he left me out because of my personal problems. In hindsight I am glad that I was not chosen, but at the time it looked like a great job to be on. I do remember that the team were picked with great care. The location and objective were kept secret, even from the rest of the troop. Only when they returned did we learn of the actual details, by which time it was plastered all over the media.

In late 1987 a well-known IRA bomb-maker, Sean Savage, was tracked down in Spain, along with Daniel McCann, another IRA suspect. MI5 spent the next six months watching the two, gathering information that they were certain was leading to a bombing. When, on 4 March 1988, Mairead Farrell arrived at Malaga airport and was met by the two men, it seemed likely that the bombing was on. At this stage the SAS were invited to send in a team. The Gibraltar police were informed of the operation, and instructed that the IRA active service unit was to be apprehended.

For a while contact with the IRA cell was lost, but by this time the target had been defined. It was suspected that a car would be delivered on to the Rock and parked somewhere along the route due to be taken by a military parade. This vehicle would be clean – a dummy to guarantee a parking space for the real car-bomb. The best spot to cause the most damage seemed to be the Plaza, where troops and the public would assemble. This proved to be correct. At 1400 hrs on 5 March a report was received that Savage had been spotted in a parked white Renault 5, possibly setting up the bomb-triggering device. Not long afterwards, Farrell and McCann were seen crossing the border from Spain and making their way into town.

Robbo and his team were immediately deployed and, once Savage was out of the way, an explosives expert walked past the Renault. No tell-tale signs of the presence of a bomb were observed, such as the rear suspension being depressed. However, if they were using Semtex, 30 lb or more could be easily concealed from the naked eye. After consultation, it was considered probable that the car did contain a bomb.

At this stage the local police chief, Joseph Canepa, signed an order passing control to the SAS. Operation Favius, as it was known, was about to be concluded. The orders stated that the SAS were to capture the three bombers if possible. But as in all such situations, if there is a direct threat to life, be it to the SAS or anyone else, they had the right to shoot. It was stressed that the bomb would more than likely be fired from a push-button detonator.

So, dressed in casual clothes, and keeping in contact via small radios hidden about their person, the SAS men, each armed with a 9mm Browning Hi-Power, shadowed the terrorist. Savage met up with McCann and Farrell, and after a short discussion all three made their way back towards the Spanish border. Four SAS men continued to shadow the trio. Suddenly, for some unexplained reason, Savage turned round and started to make his way back into the town. Our guys split: two went with Savage and two stayed with McCann and Farrell.

A few moments later, fate took a hand. A local policeman, driving in heavy traffic, was recalled to the station. It was said later that his car was required; whatever, in order to get there quickly he activated his siren. All this happened close to

McCann and Farrell, making the pair turn nervously. McCann made eye contact with one of our men, who was no more than 10 yards away. In response the soldier, who told me this story himself, was about to issue a challenge. McCann's arm moved distinctly across his body. Fearing that he might detonate the bomb, the SAS team guys fired. McCann was hit just below the nose, snapping his head back; the second round took him through the throat. Farrell made a movement for her bag. Our guys, fearing she was going for a gun or presser switch, fired. She was shot with a single round. By this time a back-up man had drawn his pistol and also opened fire, hitting both terrorists.

On hearing the shots Savage had turned, only to be confronted by the other two men. A warning was shouted this time, but Savage continued to reach into his pocket – both men fired and Savage was killed.

As the first reports of the event came through to the media it looked like a professional job, but the euphoria was short-lived. No bomb was found in the car, and all three terrorists were discovered to have been unarmed. Although a bomb was later traced in Malaga, the press and the IRA had a field day. Allegations were made, and witnesses were found who claimed to have seen the whole thing. The trio had surrendered, their arms had been in the air; they had been shot at point-blank range while they lay on the ground, and so on.

Not for the first time the SAS were held up as killers. No matter that they had probably saved the lives of many people. As I said, I am glad I didn't get the job. When the guys returned they were really put through the mill, and eventually appeared at the inquest in September 1988. It lasted two weeks and eventually a verdict of lawful killing was declared.

Although this satisfied most people, the story did not end there. The SAS soldiers who had taken part in the shooting in

Gibraltar were taken to court by relatives of the three IRA members killed. The European Commission of Human Rights in Strasbourg decided that the SAS had not used unnecessary force. They declared that the soldiers had been justified in opening fire as the IRA members were apparently about to detonate a bomb. However, they did refer the case to the European Court of Human Rights. As a result of this court case, the British government was forced to pay heavy compensation.

As for me, I had enough personal problems to keep me going. I was getting so much hassle in camp that Tara and I decided to buy a home of our own in Hereford. Unfortunately, we purchased it just as house prices peaked; and then came the recession. We struggled with the mortgage for about eighteen months, hoping that something would happen, but June was pressuring me for money all the time and our financial situation just got worse.

The families officer supported June. The way the regiment looked at it, I had been having an affair and left my wife with two young children, one of whom was disabled and terminally ill. They didn't take into consideration the fact that when I was on station I had the boys every Wednesday and every weekend, or the fact that June was going out with whom she liked. When Tara and I moved into the new house I thought that this would help provide a better life for us and the boys. I was feeling increasingly anxious about the boys and I thought that one day they would probably come to live with us permanently.

After my divorce came through Tara and I got married, but I was away for much of 1989 and when I returned it was to an empty house. A while earlier, Tara had decided to leave the army, and she had now started training for a career in the fire service. Neither of us realised what appalling sex discrimination she would have to face.

At that time there were no operational female fire fighters, so the training officers had little notion of a woman's strengths and weaknesses and made no allowances. Sheer guts and determination saw her through until the fourth week, when she and her fellow recruits were practising carry-downs: each fire fighter had to pick up a 12 stone dummy from the top of a 50-foot-high tower, climb out on to a ledge and carry it down a ladder to the ground. She could not do it to the training officer's satisfaction, and failing this test was to bug her for the rest of her career.

What amazed me was that the recruits were never shown how to do carry-downs, but had only received a verbal explanation. I was used to army training, which always follows a principle known as EDIP: explanation, demonstration, imitation, practice.

In late 1989 Tara was posted to Hereford fire station, where she was warned that her superiors were strongly opposed to the presence of women in the service. She felt like an alien in a masculine workplace.

Over the next few months I noticed a marked personality change in Tara, who became very insular and lost much of her femininity. She felt that she had to try to become one of the lads in order to hold her own in a hostile environment. It was clearly a defence mechanism, but whatever its purpose it played havoc with our relationship. She became short-tempered and paranoid and lost her smile, something that she was never to regain during our time together. We were having to support two households, and in the end we lost the house that we had bought together. Fortunately, however, we still had regular contact with the boys.

3

SOUTH AMERICA TO THE GULF

I n hindsight, the Gulf War was on the cards way back in July 1990. While Saddam Hussein prepared for final talks between Iraq and Kuwait regarding Baghdad's claims against the emirate, he was also preparing his invasion force, ready to pounce the moment the talks were over. Washington had seen through the ploy and was sending out strong signals to the world that it had adopted a general policy of non-intervention in conflicts between other nations. The Republican Senator Alfonse D'Amato's was the only voice to denounce the Iraqi leader as 'a butcher, a killer, a bully. Some day we're going to have to stand up to him. Why not now?' But we were living in a new world, one in which the Cold War had ended. International cooperation and compromise had become more fashionable than confrontation, and the USA had no wish to play the role of universal soldier. Kuwait must have looked like easy pickings to the Iraqis.

History too was on their side: the US administration had vetoed any congress-approved action against Iraq following the gassing of civilians during the Kurdistan offensive. Despite adverse reports by the Washington-based Middle East Watch organisation, the Bush administration continued to regard Saddam as one of the good guys. Influential American rightwingers admired his strong Baathist regime with its proven anti-fundamentalist credo. The only concern, if there was one, focused on Iraq's efforts to acquire nuclear and missile technology. Britain's view of Saddam was less trusting, especially after the 'supergun' affair in the spring of 1990 had become international news. Even with this reservation, both the United States and Britain accepted that Iraq had been militarily weakened by eight years of war against Iran. The only real threat to peace in the Middle East still lay with the Arab–Israeli conflict.

Such was the state of play when Iraq started its huge build-up of forces on the Kuwaiti border. Saddam was regarded by the West as at worst a third world tyrant, and at best a leader who could maintain some stability in the Middle East. In the summer of 1990 few saw him as a threat to world peace. Saddam pointed out the consequences of conventional war should America decide to intervene in what was, after all, strictly an Arab affair. He estimated that ten thousand US soldiers would die during any conflict, and the threat of terrorist action in America itself was almost guaranteed. At the same time he accused the Kuwaitis of being the aggressors by pushing down world oil prices to the detriment of the Iraqi people. By 1990 Iraq had embarked on a weapons programme that would eventually lead to nuclear parity with Israel, with missiles capable of reaching southern Europe. Though suffering short-term economic problems, Iraq had become a potential major power and had the fourth largest army in the world. In the end it was agreed that President Hosni Mubarak of Egypt would arrange a high-level meeting in Saudi Arabia between the two sides, in the hope of finding a solution. Three days later Iraq invaded Kuwait.

In August 1990, while all this was going on, we were already into our build-up training for an operation in South America. The powers that be had decided that an SAS force should help train anti-narcotics police, which would allow them to carry out their own special operations within a jungle environment. We would cover basic jungle tactics plus a few counter-terrorist methods. We were not the first – two other SAS squadrons had already been out there – but our team was the largest so far.

We had already identified the best means of dealing with our trainees and what we were going to teach them. Because they were police we would treat them as civilians, because they would have no real concept of military-type operations. The idea was to introduce a training package that would teach them all the basics, fieldcraft and weapon handling, and slowly build up to a decent standard in military tactics. We were scheduled to be in South America from late August until 17 December. This gave us three full months for training and three weeks for a test exercise. That final exercise was vital, to confirm that the police had learnt everything that we had taught them.

The Iraqi invasion did not change the regiment's plans for the South American operation. Somewhat disappointed, we prepared to spend three and a half months out there and possibly miss the war in the Middle East. The guys were really pissed off at the thought of not being involved in what would possibly be the biggest piece of action since World War II. At that stage, nobody could really have foreseen the length of time it was going to take for the generals to get everything into place, or the huge number of troops that would be required.

We flew out from RAF Lyneham on a C130 transporter, making a stop-over at Kingston, Jamaica. It was a good night out and most of us had thumping headaches as we boarded the aircraft next morning. At our final destination we were met by British Embassy officials, and at first there seemed to be a few problems because this was apparently a covert operation. Although the authorities knew why we were there, news of our arrival was kept secret. This was a little surprising: the anti-drugs campaign had been widely publicised by the Americans, and everyone knew that the British were getting involved. Margaret Thatcher, then Prime Minister, had publicly stated that she was going to send special forces to assist with the problem. The Americans funded a large percentage of the operation, and we supplied about £60,000 worth of equipment. The overall budget was in the region of £2 million for the two-year period.

We were taken by coach to where we would be operating; it was an odd place, about 6000–7000 feet above sea level in the Andes. It took a little while to get used to, but it was great for fitness training. We spent the first three or four days reconnoitring various locations and getting the equipment sorted out. Lecture packs had already been prepared back in Hereford, but needed a little rearranging to suit the areas we would be working in.

Once we were ready, ninety or so police officers arrived to begin instruction. At this point I had my first disagreement with a sergeant called Mel – albeit a professional disagreement. Little did I know then, but it was to be the first of many both here and in the Gulf. He was expecting the students to carry out weapon training tests without first being taught the correct drills. I had had plenty of experience training recruits with the Royal Green Jackets, and tried to tell him that it would be a waste of time doing the tests first. But he wouldn't listen, and as a result we lost a full morning's training.

Despite what other books say concerning the role of the SAS in South America, the regiment did not carry out any operations against the drugs cartel. We would go out on exercises in the areas where the cartel were most active, but there was no direct confrontation. The nearest we got to some real shooting was when the Special Boat Service, who had accompanied us, reported that they were being threatened. The SBS's task had been to train some of the police in the use of boats, which would enable them to intercept shipments of drugs. One day the SBS arrived at our camp with the news that the cartel were about to attack them. Great! We were all for setting up an ambush using the SBS as bait, and giving them a taste of real war. But the OC didn't think this was a very good idea, and in the end he just moved the SBS guys to a safer location. That was the end of any real excitement during the South American trip – well, almost.

One evening when we were getting ready to go down for a weekend among the fleshpots of the city, a policeman shot one of his colleagues. Luckily these two were nothing to do with our training package – they were fully trained police officers who had been messing about in the hallway playing cops and robbers. One of them pulled his pistol and accidentally shot his friend in the head. Two of our medics tried administering first aid to the dying man, as they are trained to deal with major trauma casualties. But he had major skull and brain damage and it was quite obvious that he wasn't going to survive – even if he had, he would have been a cabbage for the rest of his life. In fairness to the medics, they tried getting some drips into him in the hope that they could save his life, but the local police didn't really want to know. Eventually they bundled the guy on to a sheet, picked him up and ran off in the direction of their rather inadequate medical centre. Then they threw him on to the back of an open vehicle and drove him 40 miles to a hospital. Surprise, surprise: by the time they arrived he was dead.

On our returning to the UK, we discovered to our delight that we would be going out to the Middle East. It seemed that the generals needed more time to gather their forces, and we had not missed the war after all. Back at camp, the whole place was one massive hive of activity. Iraq's invasion of Kuwait was a challenge that the world could not ignore. If it were to escalate into a major war, it was obvious that the SAS would be a cog in the Coalition war machine.

After the initial invasion, the Iraqis quickly built up their forces in Kuwait. At this stage the condemnation directed at Iraq was still all verbal. At the same time the Western military powers had started to look at their contingency plans, and the ball was defiantly rolling. The regiment had already ordered certain of its members to be prepared to move, and plans were under way to get them into the war zone as soon as possible. We all knew the real reason for going into Iraq: it was all down to Arab oil. Under the desert lay more than half the world's oil reserves, and such a conflict had long been planned for.

We were not certain what our role in the Gulf would actually be. At first we envisaged some kind of hostage rescue work, but by the time the SAS arrived the rescues were over. Those hostages who had been seized in Kuwait and used by Saddam Hussein as human shields had either been let go or, as rumour had it, rescued by American special forces. Most of the hostages were civilians working for American or European companies, together with a fair number of Japanese. The women and children were shipped off to hotels in Baghdad, while the men were split up and sent to various vital Iraqi war production installations. This was not a smart move by Saddam Hussein, and every country in the world condemned his actions. To have attempted to rescue the hostages on any large scale would not have been a viable option: the specialist manpower and logistics required would not have justified the risk. In the end, Saddam released the hostages before the war started. I think he realised that the Coalition would bomb the targets anyway, hostages or no hostages. After all, what are a few lives compared to the mass destruction caused by chemical warfare?

While hostages were flying home, and the chemical facilities were being totally destroyed by the air force, we were on our way to Brize Norton in Oxfordshire. We flew to the Middle East by Galaxy, an incredible aircraft which lifted the whole squadron in one go. That meant fifty men plus associated personnel, twenty vehicles, sixteen bikes, ammunition, bergens and a ton of other items.

On landing we quickly unloaded our kit and heavier equipment and were taken by truck to a place known as Victor. Victor was a very large warehouse which had previously been used for storing dates, but for the next few weeks it would be home. In a situation like this the first thing to do is to grab a bed space, which is a bit like staking your claim in the old Wild West days. You all rush in, usually sticking close to your mates, and grab the nearest set of empty beds. Once your bergen and belt kit are on it, it's yours. While this scrummage is going on the OC is shouting out some kind of welcome message while the RSM or SQMS is screaming obscenities about keeping the place tidy. 'Yeah, yeah. Heard it all before. Where's the fucking cookhouse? I'm starving.' You have to get your priorities right: grab a bed, get some food, then we can talk about fighting.

Whatever our task was to be, it looked very likely that it would be mobile. The squadron was divided into mobile fighting columns, for which we would be doing three weeks' training here in the United Arab Emirates. It fell to mobility troop to teach the rest of the boys the basic driving skills required in the desert. The hardest part was trying to train the guys who would be using the bikes; it requires a lot of concentration and skill to control a motorbike in the desert.

When you join mobility troop you go through various periods of training and have to be able to drive almost anything on wheels or tracks. Where motorbikes were concerned we were lucky: 3 Troop of A Squadron have some of the best bike riders in the British army. But being competent is one thing; riding your bike at night in extreme weather and impossible desert terrain is another. A Squadron were the only squadron to use bikes during the Iraqi operation – because we saw a use for them and had some very capable riders. We had an interesting time in the UAE, knowing that we would be fighting soon, and the guys really got their act together. We looked a mean, professional bunch.

On 17 January, as we were putting the final touch to our training, nearly 500 kilometres to the west a squadron of American Apache helicopters were about to launch the Coalition's first major attack. It was no ordinary assault, but designed to knock out the Iraqi early warning system. Devastating in its savagery, it was also designed to let Saddam Hussein know exactly what real war was about. Around 2a.m., eight Apaches armed with Hellfire missiles and multiple chain guns streaked over the Saudi border heading for Baghdad. Passing over the Iraqi ground defences, this potent war machine skimmed the surface of the desert. Thirty minutes later, firing from a range of some eight kilometres, the commander gave his orders.

In the lead Apache, the pilot spoke into his microphone. 'Target ahead. Assume formation.' Immediately all eight choppers lined up facing north. Settling down in a suitable position in a small fold in the floor of the desert, they reduced their speed almost to a hover. Using the vast array of on-board vision aids, which included laser tracking and magnified infrared television, the targets at the first Iraqi radar station were selected.

'WAS to Missile,' said the leader, and the gunner selected the missile position on the fire control panel.

'Missile selected,' came the reply.

'Dropping the box,' the leader said, indicating to his gunner that the auto-hover had been engaged.

'All aircraft, tally targets. Fire at will.'

'Lasing now. Have loball now.' The gunner observed the painted laser reflection as it beaded brightly around the radar dish on the horizon. 'I have a lock. Call the ball.'

'Fire.'

There was a flash as the first Hellfire missile launched. Then, like a battery of cameras going off, the flash was repeated over and over again. The Apaches were quickly enveloped in a cloud of smoke and dust. The lead pilot eased his machine forwards clear of the clouds to give himself a clear view of the target.

At the radar station the Iraqi soldiers had been going about their business, totally oblivious of the imminent carnage. The first Hellfire ripped through the installation like a tornado, and only seconds later several more exploded. In less than two minutes the whole place was one great fireball with men running everywhere. They had not seen the Apaches; they never knew of their existence. Out in the desert the helicopters moved in for the second attack. Twenty minutes later, Iraq's two main air defence systems were almost totally destroyed. There was now a gap in their defences which would enable Coalition bombers to get through to Baghdad. The air war had begun.

We were woken at around 0600 hrs to hear the news that Allied aircraft had started bombing Baghdad and north Kuwait. This had obviously been kept very secret, and came as a total surprise to us. We were still in the United Arab Emirates, some 500 kilometres to the east, sitting in Victor Camp watching it all on CNN television. The programme gave a running commentary and showed the fighter bombers taking off. Everybody seemed to be running, and you could taste the buzz of excitement in the air. It looked like the Allies were about to bomb the shit out of Iraq – bombing which, the commentator said, was being directed by lasers operated by special forces. But in fact there were no special forces on the ground carrying out such operations at that time.

Later that morning, while we were all waiting for lunch, Brigadier Massey, who was Deputy Director Special Forces, gathered us all in the cookhouse. A, B and D Squadrons were all there, making it the strongest concentration of SAS troops since World War II. Massey climbed on to the large table in the middle of the cookhouse and asked us to gather round. This was a personal thing – something Massey always did when he was going to address the boys. Apparently it was what Monty used to do, having the men close around him as if to share a confidence. For my part, I would rather he had cut the theatricals and just told us straight what was happening.

He started by informing us about the Allied aircraft raids – but we all knew about them already as CNN and every other channel were pumping it out non-stop. Then he went on to tell us that General Sir Peter de la Billiere, known to us all as DLB, had had a meeting with the US commander, Norman Schwarz-kopf, that night and had sworn him to secrecy. Schwarzkopf had asked the US special forces commander when his men would be ready to go in. The American SF commander didn't really have an answer other than around two to three weeks, but added that he doubted whether they would be able to sustain an operation for very long. Whatever reasons he gave, Schwarzkopf was not a happy man. He turned to DLB and asked the same question. DLB briefly discussed it with Massey, then said, 'We can be in the forward mounting base tonight, moving across the border the following night.'

'How long can you stay there?' Schwarzkopf asked.

'For as long as you want. Providing we can get constant supplies to the men, they will stay in indefinitely. They can live off their vehicles, or out of their bergens with a two-week re-supply schedule.'

'You fucking serious?' the Gulf commander replied.

'Yes, sir.'

'It's all yours. Don't fuck up. Good luck!' Schwarzkopf replied to DLB and Massey. The SAS were in the war – not only that, but we were going to knock on Saddam's front door. As Massey explained this to us, it gave us all a great sense of importance. We, and nobody else, had been trusted with a special job. Massey went on to say, 'Gentlemen, you're going in from tonight. Moving into the biggest theme park the world has ever seen, and you are the only ones invited to the opening. You can go in there and enjoy yourselves – do whatever you need to do. Cause as much hassle and chaos as you like.'

So we were off. Everything was ready: kit packed, vehicles packed, my bike ready to go. D Squadron were first in the lift, then it was our turn. We had our own RAF special forces flight, which operated day and night. The moment they had dropped one load off they would return, loading up more vehicles and troops before heading north-west to an air base in Saudi Arabia.

It was dark, around 2200 hrs, when we took off for Saudi. I immediately made a beeline for the flight deck. The great thing about the pilots of SF aircraft is they don't mind the guys sitting up there with them. You can grab a set of headphones and listen to them chatting to base while they are flying the aircraft. I got myself a prime position with a couple of other lads from the troop for what was to be the most memorable flight of my career – especially when we were within thirty minutes of landing and the sky suddenly came to life. There were Allied aircraft everywhere, like bright fireflies against the pitch-black desert night. The sky seemed alive with the tail lights of warplanes of every description moving backwards, forwards and sideways, all with one common purpose: most were either going on, or returning from, a visit to Iraq. With so many aircraft flying, Saddam must have been reeling from this second night of bombing. Through my headset the radio was buzzing with British, American, French and Arabic-speaking voices. It was an awesome flying demonstration, orchestrated by the AWACs flying above.

Closer to the Saudi–Iraqi border it was like a powerhouse. As they crossed the border going in, the aircraft would turn off their lights. On returning, the lights would go on at the same point. I know this was war, but words cannot describe the beauty of the spectacle. To add to the wonder, we were then treated to 'St Elmo's Fire', the phenomenon of static electricity across the windscreen of the aircraft like something from a Spielberg movie. Then we were there, coming in for our landing.

The C130 taxied around to the point at which we were to offload. I went down into the cargo hold to get my bike, ready to move off the moment the aircraft came to a halt. As the huge plane swung around the load master started to lower the tailgate, and to our amazement there were soldiers everywhere outside on the pan, all running. Even in the blackout shapes were visible dashing all over the place. As the din of the aircraft's engines started to die down we realised why – we could hear air raid sirens. Seconds later someone was shouting that we should disembark as quickly as possible. No problem. In troop training we had practised a full de-bus from an aircraft in seconds. We were off like a Scud missile – which was, of course, what the air raid was about. Scuds had just been launched against Israel for the first time.

We were not sure what the hell was really going on, but many of the soldiers stationed at the air base were behaving like headless chickens. Most were Americans dressed in full NBC (nuclear biological and chemical) suits with respirators. Moving away from the C130, we watched the chaos all around. One of the NBC-clad lunatics came hurtling past us shouting in a muffled voice behind her respirator. Yes, it was a woman soldier. 'Hey, you guys! Hu, hu, hu.' I think she was trying to say, 'Gas, gas, gas.' 'There are Scuds inbound,' she gasped, and then she was gone.

We started wondering what we should do. A couple of guys had kindly taken our bikes for us, so my mate Alistair and I just sat down on a pile of our bergens next to a load of tents. We thought we should put our respirators on. Then, looking at each other, we just laughed. 'Nah, fuck it. Let's get a brew on instead!' I started to pitch my sleeping bag against someone's tent while Alistair got the tea going. Sleeping bags out, brew in hand – it's one of the first things you learn as a soldier, especially in the SAS. If you get a chance to get your head down, do it, because you never really know when your next gonk (sleep) is coming from.

We lay there and after a while the sirens stopped and the chaos died down, and people started to take their respirators off. Some young British squaddie who had obviously been attached to us came around with a message that everybody had to start taking the NAPS tablets which we had been given. They come in packets that look like contraceptive pills but the tablets are ten times bigger, and one a day was supposed to protect you against nerve agent poisoning. We each took a packet out of our respirator case and popped one. Alistair remarked, 'Fuck knows what will happen now – we'll probably get pregnant or something. Nobody knows what these things do to you!'

'Al, you might even start growing hair on your chest.'

'Fuck off.' Alistair was famous in the troop for not being able to grow facial or any other body hair. This looked funny as hell when we had been on operations for two months and not had a single shave. Everyone else was like a bear with a huge long beard, but Alistair would just have a few little black bristles sticking out – and I swear even those would blow off in a strong wind.

We finished our brews and just lay there waiting in the cool night air, not knowing what to expect. As time passed we both went quiet, drifting away into our own thoughts. That night, as on every other night I spent in Iraq, I said a little prayer to myself. Just before we drove off on our nightly hunt, or just before I went to sleep, without fail I would offer a prayer for my family and loved ones. I admit that deep down I was scared, and added a little prayer for my own safety.

Our half-squadron fighting column, with the call sign Alpha Three Zero, would be fighting behind the lines just like the original World War II SAS back in David Stirling's time. The main difference was the firepower we carried – enough to take on and destroy just about anything we could find. Hopefully, whatever mayhem we caused would force the Iraqis to deploy large forces in order to locate us, just as Stirling had achieved with the Germans in North Africa.

The fighting vehicles in our column consisted of eight Land Rovers type 110, most of which were armed with a Browning .5 heavy machine gun. Additional weapons included GPMGs, American Mark 19s, 40mm grenade launchers and Milan anti-tank missiles. Since most of our fighting would take place during the hours of darkness, we mounted the night sight for the Milan, called a MIRA, on top of one wagon which was fitted with a roll-bar. This proved to be an excellent bit of equipment. We also carried with us a variety of thermal imaging sites. All the vehicles had petrol engines which fed off two ten-gallon tanks; in addition we carried sixteen jerry-cans, giving us an operating distance of about 600 kilometres. Each wagon carried six water jerry-cans and enough rations to last us fourteen days. The normal allocation of ammunition was around 1000 rounds per man, four high explosive grenades and two white phosphorus. There were also between four and six bar mines per vehicle. In each column a Mercedes Unimog was used as the mother vehicle and carried the bulk of the stores. The Unimog's great advantage is that it can be loaded to the gunwales and still go anywhere. And it most certainly was loaded, with extras of every variety: rations, fuel, ammunition for a wide range of weapons, NBC equipment and spares.

Our orders were to take our column some 400 kilometres into Iraq. Here we were to hunt in the southern central region, making our way slowly up to the River Euphrates. Morale was high. It was the type of role the SAS are well suited to, and contact with the enemy would be on our terms and not theirs. The evening before we moved out it suddenly dawned on us that this was real. We knew where we were going, and we knew we would find serious trouble. Friends who had been allocated to different columns shook hands and cracked the odd joke. Others sat around, checked their personal equipment and secreted their blood money about their person. Blood money was standard SAS issue and consisted of gold sovereigns and what was called a blood chit – a document in English, Arabic and Farsi which promises the sum of £5000 to anyone aiding a British soldier. Each blood chit carried a unique serial number that could be checked against the person's name. I don't recall anyone ever using his blood chit, but the gold was different. On some occasions the sovereigns were regulated and each soldier had to sign for them; but at other times they were just given a fistful of gold and told to get on with it. In fairness, some of the guys did genuinely use the money to buy vehicles to aid their escape, and in battle equipment does get lost. But a lot of the gold did not turn up again at the end of the war, and since the accountability was so poor many of the guys still have their sovereigns. Good luck to them, I say.

As with any real SAS operation, the amount of personal equipment we carried was vast. Going on exercise is one thing, but when you play for real you need heavy firepower. I carried an M16 assault rifle fitted with a 40mm M203 grenade launcher. For personal protection I also carried a Browning 9mm pistol. Back-up consisted of about fifteen thirty-round magazines and a dozen grenades for the 203 launcher. Tucked away on the back of my belt kit was a good personal medical pack and a survival kit. Escape and evasion could soon become a reality. The fifteen gold sovereigns with which I was issued I stuck to some black masking tape. Next I cut the lining of my trousers and threaded the tape into my waistband. The silk escape map which we had all been given I tacked to the back of my windproof smock, where it remained until the war was over. The only identification on me was my ID tags hanging around my neck. Armed and equipped to the hilt, I still found room for one special item, a Welrod silenced pistol. At the last moment I thought this might come in handy if some Iraqi sentry needed taken care of quietly.

The initial briefing we received was useless. Intelligence said it would be warm, so many of the men were ill prepared for the worst winter the Middle East had ever encountered. Intelligence on the enemy was also very scanty. It was known that the Iraqi Republican Guard were well equipped and trained to a high standard, yet there was very little information about the rest of the army or their locations. So much for all the money we spent on spy satellite technology. In fact it made little difference: once we were deep behind enemy lines, no matter what we encountered we were going to waste it. It was planned that we would make our way north to a location where we could observe the Saudi–Iraqi border. Then we were to find a place to cross the border, which at this stage, so intelligence had informed us, was one huge minefield.

When we set out the weather had already started to change. It was getting very cold at night, and the mist slowed us down. I knew we had some distance to go, but after two days' driving we still hadn't reached the border. This was mainly due to bad intelligence and the fact that we were being very cautious: there's no point in driving straight at a minefield. By the time we stopped on the second night it was about 0139 hrs and we were all very tired. All except Pat, who never seemed to tire despite the weight of command and doing most of the recces.

Pat was a quiet sort of guy, but very stable and a great influence on everyone, especially me. He was slim and stood over six foot tall, and his head was topped with silvery hair despite the fact that he was only in his mid-thirties. The first thing you noticed about him was his voice. Pat was extremely well spoken and well educated, and had a natural gift for languages. He should have been an officer. Throughout my time in the SAS, he was the calmest man I have ever worked with.

That said, at the moment Pat was getting a bit frustrated – as indeed we all were: we should have been well over the border by now. Pat stopped the column and decided that we should do a recce on bikes. Climbing out of the wagon he came round to my side. 'Yorky, get your spyglass – we're off on a recce. Okay, mate?'

'No problem.' I went in search of a bike, and twenty minutes later we were ready to go.

As we set off, the other guys in the column were already getting their heads down and sentries were posted. So far none of us had much sleep, and we were all feeling a bit on edge. Pat and I took off into the unknown, racing our bikes into the darkness. It was the first of many such recces we would do together. New ground for both of us, it was like something out of a movie – just the two of us on motorbikes speeding across the desert towards a real enemy. The bikes were very manoeuvrable, and we had plenty of personal firepower including a couple of 66mm rockets. In addition I had taken the Spyglass thermal imager strapped to the bike. We worked out a route that would be good for the vehicles, checking for any major obstacles. Every so often we stopped to give me time to observe with the thermal imager and check that the way ahead was clear.

After riding for about two hours we spotted a large sand bank to our front. This was it – the border between Saudi Arabia and Iraq. Astride the bike, I checked once more with the thermal imager. The Iraqi engineers had constructed a massive ditch system and built a sand bank with the spoil. Throughout our time in Iraq we saw many such constructions, which we named 'burnes'. This one was about 15 feet high and 20 feet thick – a major obstacle for the vehicles. When we checked, it seemed all clear. Kick starting the bikes, we moved forwards towards the burne, stopping at its base. Cutting the engines once more, we dismounted. I grabbed my M16 with its 203 grenade launcher, just in case we needed a little firepower. For some reason I recall gripping the rifle very tight. At times like this you must be ready for anything. I felt really good: systems at 100 per cent. If the enemy had appeared at that moment, they would have been breakfasting in Valhalla.

Slipping the spyglass over my shoulder, as I would need it to observe the enemy, we started for the top of the burne. Pat moved up first, with me a metre behind. The sand was loose and gave way under our feet. Three steps forward, two steps back. We finished up running just to stay in the same place. Reaching the top, we both crouched in order to keep our silhouettes as small as possible. Even so, we were aware that we were breaking one of the basic rules of concealment. In the end we gouged a groove out of the sand which lowered our profile further, and set about observing the enemy positions. There it was: our first glimpse of the Iraqi war machine. There were antennas, armoured vehicles, soldiers in trenches, and all of this no more than 100 metres away. I swung the spyglass left and right. The horizon shook with activity. Every now and then the spyglass would identify the red-hot images of Iraqi vehicles moving around. Quickly flicking the switch from wide angle to zoom, I refocused. 'Shit, Pat, there are fucking thousands of them out there.'

'Give me a quick look.' Pat was excited and wanted to see for himself.

'Hang on. Let me check it all out first,' I insisted, reluctant to be distracted from my observations. I could make out the images of a group of men next to some vehicles, which changed the display from red-hot to black-hot. The imager recognises heat, which is shown in black, while the cooler areas appear as red/orange or even white, depending on the temperature. Thousands of men were walking carefully around as though they were camping, but from my view they looked very spooky. Through the imager I saw figures with black heads, eyes, chests, armpits and crotches, and the rest of their bodies in varying shades of red, orange and white. Again it dawned on me where I was and what I was doing. I have to tell you I'm no hero, and at that moment my insides started to feel very scared.

If Pat noticed he didn't show it, but just whispered a few words of encouragement. 'They're just conscripts, Yorky. They're men like you and me. You shoot them and they bleed.' We watched the Iraqi movements for a little longer, then Pat spoke again. 'Yorky, I don't think we should cross here, do you?' His voice was very matter of fact, and I wasn't sure if he was making a joke or not.

I looked at him and said, 'Why not?' Then we both started laughing, or at least giggling silently. True to form, he had put everything in perspective. There we were, 100 metres away from the Iraqi army, laughing our tits off.

When we had pulled ourselves together we went back to work, sliding back down the bank and trying to cover the signs of our presence. We repaired the groove at the top, which in daylight would have alerted the enemy. Once back at the bikes we decided to drive up and down the line of the burne, hoping to find a gap. It seemed impossible that the Iraqis could man the whole border in such strength as we had just witnessed.

'You would have thought that intelligence could have identified a crossing point for us, Pat.'

Climbing on to his bike, he simply said, 'You should have learnt by now, Yorky. We're nothing but mushrooms, kept in the dark and fed on shit.'

We drove off. Neither Pat nor myself had had any sleep for the past three days, but the adrenaline pumping through my veins would keep me awake. We had been riding an hour when we both suddenly stopped. Something was in front of us. 'What is it?' asked Pat.

'There,' I whispered to him. 'There's fucking two of them over there by the vehicle.' I turned on the spyglass, but the shape had disappeared. 'There's nothing there. Sorry, Pat, I think I've just had a hallucination.'

'Thank fuck for that – I thought you were going mad.' But Pat knew we were totally knackered. The problem was that we had only just started the operation, and the worst was still to come. It was already daylight when we eventually got back to our vehicles.

'Go and get your head down, Yorky,' said Pat, who still had to make out his report.

'Okay,' I replied, but decided to wait a while anyway. One of the lads had made Pat and me a brew, so I decided to hang around listening to him brief the OC, Mel, Richard and Slugger. Mel looked pissed off because we hadn't found a crossing place and started talking rubbish about just driving over there, giving no thought to the strength of enemy forces that we had spotted at the burne. I butted in, saying, 'If we cross at that point we'll get mutilated.'

Mel was in his early thirties, with thinning dark hair which he seemed to be losing on a daily basis. He was not very tall, but what he lacked in height he made up for in muscle. The problem with Mel was that he was too gung-ho. I also got the impression that he thought he should be in command: he used every opportunity to try to put Pat down, especially later when Brian, the RSM, took over the column.

Pat and Slugger agreed to look for another way across, while Mel was on his own and Richard didn't say anything. The OC didn't have much to contribute and didn't really inspire confidence. I left them, went to my wagon and climbed into my green maggot, as we call our sleeping bags. Two minutes later I was sound asleep, oblivious to the activities around me.

Later that morning I was woken by one of the guys telling me I was on stag – sentry duty. When I looked at my watch I saw I had slept for no more than four hours, and I felt like shit. Moving like a zombie I got up, put my webbing on, grabbed my rifle with one hand and a cup of tea with the other, and set off for the sentry position which covered the entrance to a dry riverbed or wadi. I was there as an early warning should anything turn up. I lay down in the position, which consisted of a small dip with a few rocks placed more to provide cover from view than cover from enemy fire. Although we were still outside Iraq, we were operationally cautious and well aware that Saddam's forces might invade Saudi Arabia. Looking back, it seems quite funny. We were far more tactical in our movements before we had crossed the border than when we were holed up just some 80 kilometres from Baghdad.

Pat, Mel and Slugger had gone on yet another bike recce of the border, this time hoping to find a crossing place. They returned mid-afternoon to inform us that there were still lots of enemy over the other side of the burne. Mel, who had now seen the situation for himself, still thought it was a good idea to cross at the point that Pat and I had recced the previous night, despite being in full view of a large number of enemy.

Eventually the decision was made. We would go further east and find a safer place to cross. As we moved off that afternoon, it was clear that we were going to have command problems within the column. Mel had gone back to his vehicle and called his own troop together, briefing them on the situation and adding his opinion that Pat and the OC were wankers. He tried to make out that they were both scared of going over the border. He may have been right about the OC being scared; Pat, on the other hand, was as cool as they come – he was just being professional and sensible. If we had gone along with Mel and crossed the border where it was heavily defended, it would have been suicidal. Our mission was to infiltrate Iraq, not to take on the border defences – the Coalition air force were going to take them out with saturation bombing. I don't think Mel was being completely honest with his men, and that was just the beginning.

I had just returned from a recce with Pat, Mel and Slugger, having gone to observe the border for the third time, when we received visitors: one of our four-tonne trucks. We had been expecting a quick re-supply, but no one had informed us that it was coming today. Simon, who was the OC of the forward projection wing, had also come along for the ride. While the quartermaster sergeant immediately started dishing out water and fuel, Simon took Pat, Mel and the OC to one side. Jimmy, one of the troop staff sergeants who had also arrived with the re-supply truck, sauntered across. He told us that HQ were not happy with our progress, and definitely not happy with the OC. When I explained the position that we were in he said that HQ knew of a part of the border no more than an hour away where we could cross. From what Jimmy said, it looked like the OC and Pat were being taken there for a recce. This was great news, though why they hadn't told us this in the first place I don't know.

We immediately started getting ready in the hope of crossing the border later that night. At 1600 hrs, with two hours of light remaining, we moved down a small wadi system towards a Saudi fortress some 200 metres from the border. When we got near to the fort we thought it prudent to fly the Union Jack. We all carried these flags, more for aircraft recognition than anything else – although from anything over 5000 feet they were not easily seen. The soldiers cheered us as we approached, which made us all feel good, as if for once right rather than might was on our side. This was a feature of the Gulf War: many nations and religions joined in battle against a common enemy. Being part of the new world order made us feel virtuous.

The Saudi fortress was on high ground which overlooked the border and the Iraqi defensive positions beyond. Pat asked me to get out my spyglass and follow him once more; everyone else was to stay put.

He quickly briefed me. 'I want you to go up on to the roof of the fort and have a good look at the enemy positions with the thermal imager. I noticed that two are exactly 400 metres apart, and I've confirmed this with the laser rangefinder. See if you can plot me a route through.' By this time it was dusk, and although the light was fading fast it was an ideal time for observing the enemy fortifications. I climbed up on to the parapet and took the spyglass from around my neck, selecting 'red-hot' before crawling to the edge. I raised myself up just enough to see the Iraqi positions. There they were. I concentrated on the two that Pat had mentioned – bunkers constructed of sandbags with nothing more than a canvas roof. The spyglass indicated heat coming from the positions, which meant that there were probably men inside, but I could make out no one on the outside.

Pat came over and whispered, 'Can you see anything? Is there movement?'

'It's all clear, mate – there are soldiers in the bunkers, but little else. I'll give it a couple more minutes, just to check all round. Okay?'

'Yes, let me know when you're ready. The route we're taking is down the trench to the base of the hill and up the other side between the two positions.'

'I can make out what looks like some sort of track.' Again I felt the old fear rise up in me, as if something evil was about to happen, but Pat's reassuring voice made the demons slip away. Five minutes later I was downstairs, confirming to Pat and the OC that it was all clear.

'Okay, then let's do it,' said Pat.

As we walked out of the fortress I saw a number of Saudi

border guards looking at us in total disbelief. Back at the wagons, Pat had called the guys over and quickly briefed them. 'This is it, fellas. Let's do it. Everybody back to your vehicles.'

I was just wrapping my shamag Arab head-dress around my head when Alistair pulled up alongside on his bike. We had been friends for a long time; now, shaking hands, we wished each other luck. We had done the same the night we had split from the other half-squadron. It was a journey into the unknown. Then Alistair rode off while I remained behind the steering wheel. I turned the key and the mighty V8 engine turned over quietly. Revving very low, I put it into second gear, low ratio, and took the handbrake off. There's an old saying in mobility troop: 'Low ratio, second gear, go anywhere.' For us it was Iraq next stop.

4

FIRST KILL

We drove down in single line formation from the Saudi fort, heading for the Iraqi border: it was as simple as that. Eventually we picked up the track I had spotted. The Unimog was positioned in the middle of the column, as we couldn't afford the risk of it getting hit. The bikes rode ahead, sweeping out to the flanks and checking for any ambushes. This tactic not only prevented us from being surprised but also gave us time to get the guns into line should the enemy suddenly appear. In addition to the bikes, the lead vehicle always had a thermal imager which allowed the column to detect potential problems in advance.

I drove slowly, as the terrain in western Iraq is primarily lava bed, laced with deep-cut wadis. Getting through these proved a bit of a problem, as we were vulnerable in the low ground. Luckily for us we encountered no Iraqi ambushes. The final sight I recall was the silhouette of the Saudi fort slipping by on my left. Immediately the ground dropped away, sloping into a small wadi before rising up gradually on the other side. I could see the lights shining from the Iraqi bunkers. Initially, I had decided to drive without the aid of PNGs (passive night goggles) because I was concerned that they would interfere with my vision should we have contact with the enemy. As I neared the crest of the hill to my front, I noticed to my right another Iraqi bunker which had been concealed from view during my observations from the fort, and had a firing point which was facing in my direction. As I reached the edge of the track I was forced to slow the vehicle to a crawl, eventually stopping by a

73

sand mound. Quietly I informed Pat of the new threat, and he immediately started observing the bunker with his 'Kite site'. Mitch, who was in the back manning the .50cal machine gun, swung it round to cover the bunker and I made ready with my rifle.

'Keep going, Yorky, just keep going!'

I obeyed and continued to crawl over the mound, but I was going too slowly and the engine stalled.

Pat whispered to me, 'Out of gear. Turn the key – let's get going.' He knew I knew the drill, but in his own inimitable way he was telling me to keep calm. When I had restarted the engine, we crawled over the mound and pressed on. After that there were no further problems, and we drove between the two Iraqi positions without hearing a murmur from either of them. Soon we were out into open desert – just shadows disappearing into the darkness.

We had been driving for less than two hours when we stopped for a navigation check. At that precise moment the sound of metal hitting metal rang out: the rear vehicle had run straight into the back of Unimog. Luckily it wasn't at speed, or there might have been serious casualties. Still, the collision had wrecked the radiator on the Land Rover and shunted the dashboard over on to the passenger side, where the OC was sitting. Luckily for him, it had stopped a couple of inches from his seat. The vehicle commander had been asleep with his legs up on the dashboard, so serious injury had been avoided. He had lurched forwards, cracking his head on the machine gun. Charlie, the driver, admitted straightaway that he had dropped off to sleep, and he had no excuse other than he was totally exhausted. Some may say that there was no justification for the accident, especially just two hours over the border. However, we had been tactical for four days before reaching Iraq. In that time most of the drivers had had very little sleep, and in truth we were all totally wrecked before we made the crossing. Our excuse, if we really needed one, was that we had pushed ourselves to the limit before the operation had even begun. Still, we knew that those back at HQ who sleep each night in a comfortable bed would be swift to criticise – they don't like to admit that the SAS can make mistakes!

Our immediate concern was to get moving once more. All the mobility guys gathered around, assessing the damage. We quickly hooked up the casualty to the Unimog and towed it until we could deal with it properly when we reached our first Iraqi lay-up point (LUP).

When we got there we stopped short of the area, which consisted of a series of small hills in which we could hide. Pat and I jumped off the wagon, quickly informed the drivers of other vehicles, then patrolled up the centre of the wadi. Mitch and Matt did the same down the other side. Everything looked okay, so we returned and the column moved into the LUP. We set up the vehicles in pairs, each group training their guns to cover a different arc of fire. Following this well-rehearsed routine, we had the vehicles camouflaged in no time, and by daybreak we were settled in. Once everything was done, and sentries had been posted, I pulled my sleeping bag off the wagon and crawled into it. Bliss. 'Welcome to Iraq,' was my last thought as I fell into a deep sleep.

All too soon thunder cut through the fog in my brain. What the hell? Then my eyes opened, automatically following a horrendous whooshing noise.

'Tornados. Looks like a strike some 30 kilometres or so away.'

Even as Pat spoke, the distant rumble of high explosive reached our ears. Moments later, the dawn sky was lit by streams of bright red tracer rounds as the Iraqi anti-aircraft batteries made a futile effort to intercept the warplanes.

'Fuck, they startled me,' I grumbled to Pat, at the same time watching the two jets disappear over the distant horizon. They were flying almost on the ground, hugging every bit of cover to avoid radar detection. I climbed out of my comfortable green maggot and went looking for a brew. The sound of rolling thunder still echoed in the distance as more Coalition jets dropped their loads on Iraqi targets.

Later that day we decided that the damaged Land Rover was going nowhere, so we dug a pit and pushed the wagon into it. After jacking it up, and taking two wheels off for spares, we de-rigged it completely before concealing it with rocks, dirt and a spare camouflage net. We learnt later that D Squadron had encountered a similar problem with a broken wagon. They too had de-rigged it, but unlike us they left a few little presents for the first Iraqis to come across it: six anti-personnel mines and a huge anti-tank mine. Apparently, after the war was over somebody went back to locate it and has not been heard from since!

For the rest of that day most of the guys who were not on sentry duty got their heads down. As night fell once more we moved off, leaving the damaged Land Rover to the Bedouin.

The bikes were brilliant for locating tracks and keeping us on our route. If we were not sure, or if the ground ahead could conceal an ambush, the bikes always went in first. Soon a pattern of operating emerged. Some of the bikes would be used as scouts, while others would pass messages along the column. This not only negated the need for radio transmissions, but if the column got too drawn out in the darkness they would herd us together. When the operation started I was designated as a motorbike rider. In fact most of the senior mobility troop guys were on bikes, which allowed the other lads a chance to get used to the job. But the night before we crossed the border I was moved over to Pat's wagon because Leslie, his original driver, was useless. The first I knew about this change was when Leslie came over to me and said Pat would like a word. I found Pat sitting in his wagon, and he was fuming. It was one of the only times I ever saw Pat get angry, and angry was an understatement. 'What's up, mate? Leslie said you wanted to see me?' I inquired mildly.

'Go and get your fucking kit and move it on to this wagon before I kill that wanker,' Pat commanded. It was rare indeed for him to get angry like this.

'Why? What's he done?'

'Yorky, just do it. And while you're at it, give him a bollocking and tell him to sort his act out.'

I returned and read the riot act to Leslie. 'I'm kicking you out of Pat's wagon. Get your kit and go back to the wagon with the Mark 19. You're its new gunner. I hope your shooting's better than your fucking driving.' As it turned out later, it wasn't. Some guys in the regiment won't admit it if they fuck up, and slag off the person who pulled them up for their mistake. That is what happened with Leslie. In his version, he always blamed Pat.

After that I drove for Pat throughout the operation, apart from a few nights towards the end when Ian took over because I was so wrecked. And out of the five weeks we spent driving behind enemy lines there were only three occasions when my wagon wasn't at the front. Even that was only because Mel had gone creeping to the RSM, who was then in command, saying, 'Let me take the lead, Brian.' Unfortunately the little arse-licker didn't have a clue about satellite navigation, and on all three occasions our vehicle was called forward to take over and sort the mess out.

We had now been in Iraq for about a week and had penetrated about 100 kilometres into the country. We had sorted out a neat little routine, moving by night and resting by day. But there was one problem we had not foreseen: the weather. It was cold in Iraq – cold like nothing one could envisage. Even the mountain troop guys who had trained in Arctic Norway in the middle of winter said they had seen nothing like it. Before we went there we had been led to believe that Iraq was like any other desert, with sand, flies and sun. Instead, we were looking out on a hostile landscape littered by small dips and ravines that cut into the soil. On top of all this, the whole region was suffering the worst climatic conditions in living memory. If Churchill could get a decent weather forecast for the D-Day landings, how come we, with all our hi-tech equipment, could not predict snow in the desert? Yes, it really did snow. But since our intelligence boys had led us to believe Iraq must be like Saudi, we set off very poorly equipped for such weather. It was always cold, but at times it was bitterly cold. First my fingers started to crack at the ends – small, insignificant-looking breaks in the skin which steadily became infected and ended up pus-filled and painful. Next my face started to feel the effects; I kept tightening and relaxing my facial muscles in an effort to increase the circulation, and this helped somewhat. Then one day, while clenching my jaw, a tooth broke off; I had been gritting my teeth so tightly that eventually one of them snapped. When I returned to the UK, I had to have six months of dental treatment.

The day of our first contact with the Iraqis turned out to be a complete disaster. In the tranquillity and obscurity provided by one of our LUP sites we were sitting around happily, protected by the overhead camouflage nets and lazily passing the day. Some guys were brewing up or scoffing food, while others were sleeping. I had been cleaning my weapon and chatting to a couple of the lads. To look at us you wouldn't have thought we had a care in the world. Then all hell broke loose in the most surreal ten minutes of my life. It happened so fast that I still wonder if it was a dream or not. But you wake up from dreams, and I still live the nightmares about that day.

We had been in position since 0630 hrs, having had quite a difficult time finding a suitable place to lie up for the day. For once the weather was quite beautiful and, despite the nippy breeze, the sun shone in a clear blue sky. Apart from the odd spoon clanking against a mess tin, or the whisper of murmuring voices punctuated by a dirty laugh, the camp was in silence.

This serenity was suddenly broken by a rumbling noise – the distinctive sound of a vehicle getting closer. Most of us who were not asleep heard it. All around me swivelling heads popped up, searching to identify the threat. I looked over to my left, where Joey was in the sentry position. He had seen a vehicle heading directly towards our position and was frantically pointing over to our right. His balled fist with thumb pointing down could mean only one thing – enemy.

'Fucking hell,' I said to no one in particular. 'There's a fucking Iraqi vehicle coming towards us.'

For ten seconds it was headless chicken time. Guys grabbed weapons, tripping over each other in their attempts to get into a good firing position – you could almost taste the adrenaline. This was what we were here for, to locate, close and kill the enemy, and it was about to happen.

Professionalism soon took over. Weapon in hand ready to acquire my target, I nestled down into a good fire position. Swiftly looking round, I could see Pat getting himself behind the machine gun on the Land Rover, while Ian, who was next to me, took up position under the camouflage net. Mel was crouched to my right, and Matt was just behind me. At times like this, firepower is what it's all about. With enough of it you can take on the devil.

Amid the rush to get into position, none of us had noticed that Mitch was still sound asleep in his green maggot. Since we were unable to risk waking him, he had to stay there until I had fired the first round. Mitch likes to think of himself as Mr Cool, so it was hilarious watching him jump out of his skin.

As the vehicle drew closer there was nothing but the sound of the engine. We knew our location was not what it should be, and we had moved in hurriedly. The Iraqis must have spotted us from some distance as they drove directly into the camp area and stopped within 20 metres of us. Luckily they must have thought that we were friendly forces, not thinking that enemy troops could be so close to Baghdad.

Matt whispered from behind, 'What the fuck are they doing?'

I ignored the question and watched the driver and passenger get out. The driver then walked to the front of his vehicle and opened up the bonnet.

'Matt. Yorky. Get ready. Cover me,' said Mel. 'I'm going out to meet him.' Mel was about to play the hero.

Breaking cover, he walked out to meet them. It was incredible to see the enemy so close. The officer was a short, slightly chubby guy in his early to mid-thirties, tidy and clean-shaven. He had dark hair and the very small moustache favoured by Middle Eastern men.

Mel emerged from under the camouflage net, his weapon held to his side to prevent it being seen.

The Iraqi approached, a look of bewilderment on his face. His head-dress, a blue beret, had the Iraqi eagle emblem badge on it, and he was wearing the insignia of a captain. We discovered later that his authority was that of a lieutenant colonel or even higher. What we didn't know was that the vehicle, a Russian Gaz 69, had more Iraqi troops in the back. The officer, complete with map case and charts, continued to walk towards Mel. Not until he was three metres away did he realise we were the enemy.

Mel swung his rifle up and fired. Nothing happened. Automatically he dropped to his knees to clear the weapon stoppage, and by doing so he cleared my line of sight to the Iraqi. I fired and the man fell dead.

With that the world erupted as everyone else opened fire. Lights like starshells exploded in my brain as the rounds spat and cracked like a bushfire consuming dried-out vegetation. I saw the driver's body do a little death dance before it finally crumpled to the ground. In a rush we all broke cover together, heading towards the vehicle. It never dawned on me at the time, but we had just initiated the first contact of the ground war and the first kill of Operation Desert Storm was down to me. It was also the first time I had ever killed a man.

Following Mel and Matt, I ran round the front of the vehicle to check out the back. The first thing I saw was Mel pulling out a man who was very seriously injured. As Mel dropped him from the vehicle, an incredible jet of blood gushed from his side. Although he had been hit several times, the main damage was just above his hip. While he was still in the truck the man's body must have been in a position that stopped the flow of blood, but once he was moved the pressure was released. Blood was pumping out at an incredible rate, splattering in a large arc for a good two to three metres; some had spurted into Mel's face.

New noises distracted me from this grotesque sight, and I turned to see Sam tangling with a half-crazed survivor. Somehow he had cheated death, for the rear cab containing the soldiers was riddled with bullet holes. Sam was screaming at the Iraqi, who in turn was wailing the Arabic for 'Praise be to God'. This man was obviously glad to be alive. Sam, in total amazement, managed to pin him to the side of the vehicle with one hand and with the other push his rifle into the Iraqi's face. This action subdued the prisoner very quickly. Then he was being rushed off to the OC's wagon to be interrogated by two of our interpreters. At this point it was chaos, with men running around. Some, who had been asleep, not knowing what had happened. More importantly, most of us not really knowing what the fuck was going to happen next. The incident had all transpired in the space of just a few seconds.

Through the confusion and chaos typical of a sudden action lasting only a few seconds, I heard a horrendous noise coming from the badly shot up Iraqi whom Mel had dragged from the wagon and who was now slumped face down in the dirt. It was quite apparent that he was not going to make it. The sound of a man choking on his own blood is not a pleasant one. I took a closer look: there was blood pouring from his mouth, and his eyes were rolling around into his head. His bodily functions were letting go, and steam and stench started to rise as the mortally wounded soldier slipped rapidly and painfully into oblivion.

Years later, I often wonder what agony this man must have been going through. Mel grabbed hold of him, rolling him over to search for weapons, maps or anything that could be of use to us. It was obvious that all he had on him was a pistol, and he was in no fit state to use that. As Mel worked, I looked into the poor bastard's eyes. Fear was all I saw.

I have not forgotten that man's face, and I doubt I ever will. I often wish I had killed him there and then. But, forgetting the incident, I immediately turned my attention to the next threat – the possibility of more enemy turning up. Then lo and behold, word quickly spread from the OC's wagon that more Iraqis were on their way towards us. This snippet of information had been obtained from the prisoner, and the two linguists had no reason to disbelieve him. He just sang like a bird, pouring out numbers and locations non-stop.

'How strong is your unit?'

'About thirty thousand men.'

'Where are they now?'

'There. Just over there.'

'Holy fuck! Let's get out of here.'

We all started packing up the wagons, quickly throwing all the cam nets into the back, then piling on our bergens and ammo boxes. Once we were ready we discovered two further problems. First was the OC, mentally up at 30,000 feet and refusing to come down. He came roaring into our position like a Tomahawk missile, screaming, 'What the hell's going on?'

Pat, calm as you like, said, 'We've just had a contact, boss. There's three enemy dead and one POW.'

'Oh God, what do we do now?' our commander cried. There was no doubt in any of our minds at this stage that the OC was losing it. It had happened before in the regiment, not just to the officers but also to some of the men; they perceive the danger to be greater than it really is. I remember one of the G Squadron guys telling me about a troop officer who had lost it during the Oman war. The guys had taken a real beating from the enemy during the night, but by dawn they had prepared adequate defences. At first light, the officer in charge kept popping up his head and saying, 'They can get us from that direction!' Turning around, he repeated the phrase. At first the men thought that he was making a joke to cheer them up. Then they took a look at his eyes. An hour later, just before another major enemy assault, the officer was taken out by helicopter. The pressures and decisions of command had just been too much. But at times like this you need strong leadership. Pat was that man.

'Pack up and fuck off, boss,' he replied.

Some of Pat's calmness must have rubbed off on the OC, for next minute he came up with the idea that we should get back across the border as quickly as possible. Not a bad idea – but we were supposed to be here killing Iraqis. Driving back to HQ in Saudi Arabia would not be good for morale. Still, this was a decision for the bosses – the head-shed. So while they got to grips with that one I and a couple of the guys started sorting the bodies out. First we dragged them over to my wagon, then we set about digging a hole in the sand with the intention of throwing them into it. After 15 centimetres or so we hit trouble: the ground was rock-hard, and it seemed unlikely that we were going to get any further. So we buried them in a hole 15 centimetres deep. It looked like something out of the *Rocky Horror Show*, and, though gruesome, quite funny at the time – there were bits of body and limbs sticking out all over the place.

Still, taking into account that we were on a deniable operation (which means that the British government would not recognise our presence in the area), leaving dead bodies lying around was not a good idea. Just as we had completed the grisly task the OC came flying over and said we must take the bodies with us. He could have told us sooner.

Quickly we dug up the bodies and threw them into the back of their own Russian-built wagon. While we were doing this, the Iraqi Mel had pulled from the wagon started to moan – the poor bastard really was hanging on to life. Getting one of the guys to drive the Gaz 69 was not a problem. Almost immediately Ian put his hand up. He had an ulterior motive: the enemy wagon had a roof and it was fitted with a heater. Bearing in mind the temperatures, especially at night, Ian was no fool. We checked the mortally wounded man, who now showed no signs of life. The driver, only a young man, had been shot a number of times in both the body and head and his death had been instant. As for the commander, we threw him on last. This had nothing to do with rank – it was just the way it was. When I had shot this man the first round had hit him in the chest, spinning him towards me. The second round had hit him in the heart. It was instinct to fire several more rounds into him as I had jumped up from my position. This is something you learn early in basic training: make sure a dead enemy stays dead.

The sight of these three men lying in the back of the truck made a grotesque spectacle as I jumped into my wagon and made ready to go. The squadron commander was still flapping, standing in front with Pat and Mel and trying to decide what to do. Everybody else just got on their wagons and waited. Eventually Pat turned to me and said, 'Hey, Yorky, which way do we go?'

'Go east for about 10 kilometres, then head south, and finally west to box our last position.' It was the best I could think of.

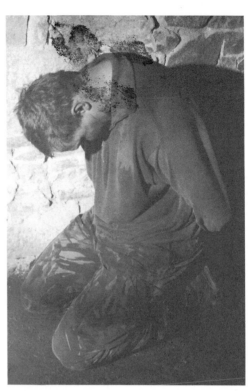

Yorky firing an mp5 on the range, dressed for the anti-terrorist team.

Undergoing interrogation training.

On combat survival training.

On escape and evasion training.

Having a beer with the boys – Yorky second from right.

During the Gulf War.

A fighting column preparing to infiltrate Iraq.

Rest period during the journey.

Note the amount of fire-power carried on the vehicle.

Taking a re-supply deep behind the Iraqi lines.

Just a few kilometres from Baghdad.

Sentry duty. Sleep and food were the priorities during daylight hours – most of the fighting took place at night.

During the Gulf War.

Dressed in Arabic winter coats as the weather became fiercely cold.

PROMISORY NOTE

HM BRITANNIC GOVERNMENT PROMISES TO PAY THE BEARER OF THIS NOTE THE
SUM OF £5000 STERLING PROVIDING YOU DO NOT HARM THE PERSON ISSUING IT
AND THAT YOU ASSIST HIM TO EITHER EVADE CAPTURE OR RETURN HIM TO EITHER
SAUDI ARABIA OR TO NEUTRAL TERRITORY. TO CLAIM THE REWARD YOU SHOULD
TAKE THIS NOTE TO ANY BRITISH EMBASSY OR CONSULATE AND ASK TO SPEAK TO
THE DEFENCE ATTACHE OR ONE OF HIS ASSISTANTS. HE WILL THEN GIVE YOU THE
SUM OF £5000.

سند اذني

تتعهد الحكومة البريطانية بالدفع لحامل هذا السند الاذني مبلغ ٥٠٠٠ جنيه استرليني شرطاً
الا تضر الفرد المصدر له وشرطاً ان تساعده في تفادى الاسر او ان تقوم باعادته الى المملكة
العربية السعودية او الى ارض محايدة . من اجل اخذ المكافأة عليك تقديم هذا السند الى سفارة
او قنصلية بريطانية وطلب الالتقاء بالملحق الدفاعي او احد معاونيه . ثم سوف يعطي لك المبلغ
المحدد اي ٥٠٠٠ جنيه استرليني . .

سند اذني

تتعهد الحكومة البريطانية بالدفع لحامل هذا السند الاذني مبلغ
٥٠٠٠ جنيه استرليني شرطاً الا تضر الفرد المصدر له وشرطاً
ان تساعده في تفادى الاسر او ان تقوم باعادته الى المملكة العربية
السعودية او الى ارض محايدة . من اجل اخذ المكافأة عليك
تقديم هذا السند الى سفارة او قنصلية بريطانية وطلب الالتقاء
بالملحق الدفاعي او احد معاونيه . ثم سوف يعطي لك المبلغ
المحدد اي ٥٠٠٠ جنيه استرليني .

A blood chit or promissory note.

Acting out an anti-terrorist role
during the making of an ITN film.

Yorky playing the lead in an SAS video to be released in late 1996.

'Yeah, that's what we'll do,' replied Pat. It was a decision – not necessarily the right one, but a decision nevertheless – and it got the OC's mind on to doing something positive. Amazingly, the more the commander lost it, the calmer Pat became. The POW was bagged and tagged, then thrown on the back of the Unimog. Then at last, some fifteen minutes after the initial contact with the enemy, we started to move away from the position. It had all been done in such a rush that we had forgotten the two guys on the sentry position. Suddenly they came hurtling down the hill, thinking that we were going to leave them behind. And we would have done, had they not taken the initiative to join us. What a fuck-up that would have been! Eventually we got rolling. Our aim was to get close to the Saudi border, which would enable us to jump over the border if we had to and also to get a scheduled re-supply more easily. In addition, it would be safer for the RAF to get the Iraqi dead and the POW out.

As planned, we continued heading east for about one hour. As darkness fell we spotted columns of Iraqi vehicles and tanks, but in the dusk we must have looked just like them. To prevent the Iraqis getting too close we avoided the road and rough tracks, cutting carefully across the barren countryside. After about two hours we stopped and Pat jumped off my vehicle to go and check on everyone. He was especially worried about Ian, who was driving the Iraqi vehicle containing all the bodies. But Pat came back with a smile on his face and said, 'Ian's as happy as a pig in shit. The vehicle stinks to high heaven, especially with the heater on full blast. But I think he'll shoot anyone who tries to take his place.'

I couldn't help feeling just a little envious. The night was bitterly cold and the sky dark and overcast with occasional rain. Driving over the rough terrain in our open vehicles, I found my concentration constantly lapsing because of the cold. The cracks around the ends of my fingers were getting worse and my summer clothing was wet through, greatly increasing the wind chill-factor.

Pat instructed me to drive on, but we had only been moving about half an hour when I noticed something through my PNGs. Because the magnification was minimal I couldn't make out what I was actually looking at, but I wasn't happy. Call it a gut feeling, but there was definitely something out there. I asked Pat to have a look with the Kite sight, which had a greater magnification.

'Fucking hell!'

'What is it?' I asked quickly.

'Have a look,' he replied.

'Fuck it. I knew there was something out there.' About 100 metres directly in front of us were about ten Iraqi soldiers carrying weapons and equipment. They appeared to be wearing full battle order complete with helmets, and had ponchos draped over their shoulders as protection against the rain. It was quite possible that their morale was very low. They were walking with their heads down, not really paying any attention to what was going on around them. Behind them were what looked like several vehicles, but we were unable to identify make or type.

Pat's head came close to mine. 'Go right.'

Just then the Milan vehicle came roaring up alongside us with one of the guys hanging off the side shouting, 'Fucking enemy! Fucking enemy!'

Pat and myself immediately turned and told the idiot to keep quiet.

'Let's get the hell out of here.' No sooner said than done. We drove for another two hours, bumping into Iraqi troops every so often. It was quite nerve-racking at first, but at no time did they react. I put this down to the darkness, plus the fact that the Iraqis seemed totally switched off. To them we were just more of their soldiers looking for our position.

Around midnight we found a location in which we could hide. It offered excellent cover from view, and good protection in a fire-fight. We arranged our defences by putting the vehicles on the higher ground, with the HQ vehicles in the centre of the position. The position itself was like a depression in the ground, big enough for the vehicles to turn, and with a good exit route should we get heavily outnumbered. Pat, the OC and Mel then started to send a contact report, relaying our situation back to HQ. While this was being done Ian, Ben and I decided to get the bodies off the Iraqi vehicle and bury them. The air in the back was now pretty unpleasant, but I must admit to lingering a little due to the welcome heat. Then, grasping one of them by the ankles, I dragged it from the truck. Ian and Ben did the same, and we dragged the three dead bodies by their feet to where some of the other guys had started digging a communal grave. The badly wounded soldier had hung on for nearly two hours in the back with his dead comrades. Ian said he could hear the man moaning and groaning while he was driving. I decided to check and found that he was now dead, poor sod. As before, the ground was so hard that we only managed to dig down some 15–20 centimetres. In order to accommodate the three bodies we made it wider, which enabled us to pile the earth and rocks over them. After placing the bodies in the ditch we had started to cover them up with dust and rocks when once more we were interrupted. The squadron commander came running over and demanded to know what we were doing. Somewhat surprised, I replied, 'We're burying the bodies!' To our amazement he ordered us to dig them up again and put them back on the vehicle. So for the second time, we uncovered the three Iraqis and returned them to their vehicle. This was getting ridiculous. Needless to say, by now the bodies were in some state.

Once the contact report had been received we moved off, continuing in a southerly direction. Pat said the intention was to get to within 25 kilometres of the border, where arrangements had been made for a re-supply from the RAF. We drove for the rest of the night, stopping just before dawn because moving around in daylight so close to the border was not a good idea. While the column waited, Pat and I went forward and located what looked like a disused Scud site. It was an ideal position to defend, so we called the rest of the column into the position and started our normal routine.

Men were sent out to watch likely enemy approach routes and to set anti-tank and anti-personnel mines along the route we had just moved in on. This was done to give us early warning if the enemy did appear. As I was the mortar fire controller, I helped Mike and Joey set it up. My next task was to plot DF (defensive fire) positions that the mortars could fire on, if and when required.

The rest of the guys started camouflaging the vehicles and getting on with their normal administration. As always, the priorities were to clean their weapons, clean themselves and then get some hot food going. Sentries were continually changed due to the cold. Any vehicle that needed repair or maintenance was seen to. The next priority was getting into the green maggot, generating some body heat and with luck getting some sleep.

As things started to relax and settle down, we started to consider once more what to do with the prisoner of war and the three dead bodies. Ben took it upon himself to look after the prisoner, while the four of us started getting the bodies out of the vehicles and putting them in body bags. This was not a pleasant task – but, looking on the bright side, it could have been the Iraqis putting us into the bags. The body bags were basically large, heavy-duty bin liners. We sealed them up and put them back on to the vehicle. That done, we spent the rest of the day feeding our faces or chewing the fat about the night's activities over a brew of tea.

Eventually I tried to snatch a couple of hours' kip, but I was about to drop off when the vision of the Iraqi officer re-appeared. Once more I shot him. My brain kept on playing this scene over and over, and each time there would be more detail. At one stage I remember looking over my sights at the man's chest and seeing his eyes burn into mine. We made eye contact just for a second, and he hated me for killing him. Years later, when I was an SAS instructor, I would relate this feeling to my students. I called it first kill syndrome – the moment in your life when you are about to take a life for the first time. But with that Iraqi I have no regrets.

The re-supply was due to fly in at 0400 hrs and at the same time pick up the bodies and the prisoner, but from experience we knew it would arrive when it arrived. When we eventually heard the sound of a Chinook in the distance, we stood to. Several minutes later, to our amazement the chopper flew straight past. Nobody knew what was going on, and because the re-supplies were done on a predesignated location basis radio silence had to be maintained. The head-shed thought that if our signals were being picked up by Iraqi location finders retaliation would follow. The only explanation we could think of was that the Chinook was going north first in order to re-supply some other SAS call sign. Whatever, we had just pushed the Iraqi vehicle out on to the landing site when the helicopter flew by, and now we had to push it back again. At least this labour kept us warm; but we were not amused. There was a lot of abuse from Ian and me, mostly directed at the RAF – not for nothing were they known as Crab-Air.

If everything went wrong, Ian, Slugger and I decided, we would push the Iraqi vehicle into a nearby ditch. Then we would put some explosives underneath and just blow it, together with the bodies. The POW we could handle. We were just about to heave the vehicle into the ditch when somebody heard the helicopter again, and so we struggled to push it back out towards the landing site once more.

The helicopter came in low and fast. No matter what we say about the crabs, the pilots of these things were very good, flying between 10 and 20 feet above the ground and using only PNGs to penetrate the darkness. This was our first re-supply and it was an amazing experience. As the chopper got closer it flared its rotors, kicking up great clouds of dust. All we could see were millions of tiny sparks created as the dust made contact with the rotor blades. Because of this friction, a kind of weird blue glow surrounded the aircraft. It looked spectacular at first, but then we started to wonder if the noise and glow would give away our position. Thank God there were no Iraqis around. But just in case, we had put three vehicles on to the high ground around our position to give us some sort of early warning and provide cover while the Chinook got away. The rest of the guys were poised ready to unload, crouching down so they didn't get blown over by the downdraught of the helicopter as it came to rest.

Once the pilot had settled on the desert floor, but with the rotors continuing to turn, the tailgate started to drop. I could see the side-door gunner sitting ready for action with his 30 calibre mini-gun. The tailgate dropped fully open and two men jumped off the aircraft, both carrying machine guns. Additionally, I could just make out the silhouette of a man standing on the tailgate. The third man appeared to have all his equipment, with a weapon in his hand and a bergen to his side. This guy was definitely SAS, but who and why?

Next I noticed Paul, our quartermaster sergeant, jumping off the chopper and shouting above the noise in an attempt to get things organised. The mystery new arrival remained on the tailgate. Then I noticed Paul saying something to Pat. Pat in turn went across to the man on the tailgate, who handed Pat what looked like a piece of paper. Immediately Pat turned and ran off towards the OC's vehicle. Something was up, I thought to myself. Who the fuck was that on the tailgate?

Paul's voice meant that the answer to my question would have to wait. First we had to get the re-supply off by hand. Six 50-gallon oil drums containing petrol and diesel were rolled off; fourteen days' rations for thirty-six men followed; then more ammunition; and what looked like a big bunch of blankets. I couldn't believe it – when you need Arctic clothing they send you a bunch of blankets! As it turned out they weren't blankets but local Arab winter coats, and they were brilliant.

Pat now came back with the OC and Mel, and soon they were deep in conversation with the mystery man on the tailgate. I was too busy ferrying jerry-cans of petrol to listen, and anyway it was none of my business. By the time I came back to the helicopter everybody had disappeared off the tailgate, but I could just see their silhouettes inside the aircraft. Paul turned and shouted, 'That's everything,' meaning that the pilot could now lift off. But Ian and I shouted in unison: 'What about the Iraqi vehicle and the dead bodies?'

Paul shook his head. 'We can't take them – just the POW.'

'What a fuck-up!' I said to Ian. 'Now what are we going to do about the vehicle and the bodies?' Some years later I got talking to the crab load-master of that Chinook. No one had told him about the vehicle or the bodies, and they would in fact have been happy to take them out for us.

Our immediate problem was handling the re-supply. Prior to the operation we had been told that fuel would come in jerry-cans and rations and other equipment in packs, allowing us just to throw them on to the vehicles. Not so: now we had to work out the quickest and most effective way of refuelling nearly two hundred jerry-cans from six oil drums with just one hand pump. There was no point in cursing – the job just had to be done. It fell to Ian and me to deal with the fuel, while Lee and a couple of other guys got on with the rations and ammunition. At times like this you can see which guys are pulling their weight and which ones are the lazy bastards. It took one and a half hours to deal with all the equipment, fuel and rations that night. Just as we were finishing, a voice behind us said in a strong Yorkshire accent, 'Right, stop fucking flapping. We dominate the high ground, so let's get the re-supply done and fuck off.' The mystery man was Brian, the RSM.

I had not seen him getting off the chopper, but others had whispered that 'Brian the Bastard' was here. He was the most hated man in the SAS. A few minutes earlier, Slugger had come over and whispered to us that the RSM had handed the OC an envelope whose contents informed him that he was being relieved of his command. It was as simple as that: pick up your kit and get on the helicopter – your career is over. If you think relieving a major of his command while on active duty is bad news, replacing him with an inadequate RSM is adding insult to injury.

Brian was in his late thirties and not a big guy – I doubt if he was more than five foot eight. He treated everything as either black or white and there was no arguing with him; he was right and that was it. Everything that we saw he would declare to be Bedouin. We would say, 'That's the enemy over there.' Straightaway, he would state the opposite. 'No, it's not. That's the fucking Bedu, that is!' Most guys in the SAS get on fairly well, but not with Brian. Apart from Mel, I don't know anyone who had a good word to say about him. After the Gulf War he received a DCM for his exceptional command and control whilst under fire. You should have seen him at Victor Two.

The OC never asked any questions or complained. He simply turned to Pat and said, 'I'm sorry, but I've been relieved of my command. I'm going back now. All the best to you and give my best to the men.' Then he walked towards the helicopter.

Once the re-supply was finished, we needed a decision on how to dispose of the Iraqi vehicle and the bodies. Eventually, Slugger and Ian got their demolition equipment out and set up two anti-tank bar mines fitted with an XM122 timing device.

FIRST KILL

They set the timers for 0530 that morning, which would give us time to get well clear of the area. We pushed the truck, with the bodies neatly laid out in the back, back into the ditch. Then we placed one bar mine underneath the vehicle and the other on top. The fuel and diesel that we hadn't used we poured in and around the truck, wedging the part-empty fuel drums around it. This would go off with devastating effect, bearing in mind that one bar mine will completely destroy a 56-ton Chieftain tank.

Once everything was ready, Pat quickly briefed us. Mounting our vehicles, we moved off in box formation: two groups of four with the Unimog in the middle. We drove from 0230 to 0500 and covered some 35 kilometres that night. When we stopped, Pat and I went forward and did a quick recce to find a position where we could lie up during the day. Just before 0530, as we were camouflaging the vehicles, everybody looked back in the direction from which we had travelled. Exactly on time there was a bright red glow on the horizon as the mines went off, followed a few seconds later by a very dull thud. The three Iraqi soldiers had just vaporised into the desolate landscape.

5

VICTOR TWO AND A LEADERSHIP CRISIS

S addam Hussein used every trick in the book to force Israel into the conflict. If he could start even a minor air war between Israel and Iraq he knew it would send shock waves throughout the Arab world. Any large-scale Israeli attack would, for example, require massive violation of Jordanian airspace. Israeli officials are acutely aware that any confrontation with Jordan would prompt Syrian intervention, and the death of Coalition forces would follow. The Iraqis even went so far as to report that large numbers of Israeli fighter aircraft had been flown into Saudi air bases. But the Coalition commander realised that, providing the attacks on Israel could be kept to a minimum, America could use its vast political strength to stop them retaliating. But it was a big gamble. Personally, I don't think the Israelis care about anyone who is not Jewish: if it means protecting their country, they are willing to lead us all into World War III and total oblivion.

Scud missiles had been landing on Israel and Saudi Arabia from the moment we had arrived from the United Arab Emirates. Despite a massive bombing campaign by the Coalition air force, they were still creating havoc. Our new orders were to locate and attack the Scuds. But with that radio message came some bad news. One of the foot patrols, call sign Bravo Two Zero, was missing. We had all discussed the possibility of escape and evasion procedures should the need arise, and I hoped the poor bastards would make it back. If forced to go on foot, my idea was to head for the nearest border, which at best would be some 120 kilometres away. Obviously the best countries to head for would be Syria or Jordan, or those friendly to the Coalition. Mind you, given the Iraqi landscape, unless you actually saw a border crossing point you wouldn't know if you had reached safety or not. I also considered heading for one of the major rivers and floating downstream to safety. Surviving the enemy was not the only problem; water and shelter were also in short supply, not to mention the freezing weather at that time of year.

In addition to the military radio, we kept in touch by listening to the news. If nothing else it broke the monotony and provided a few lighter moments during the day. For example, Iran radio reported an ayatollah as saying that Iran should not take part in the conflict, but at the same time he believed that any Muslim who killed an American would be forgiven his sins. Iraq radio called on its citizens to help in the search for Coalition pilots who had been 'downed' or crashed. The Baghdad government said it would be offering a reward of $30,000 to anyone who captured an enemy pilot. There was no mention of the SAS, so we took it that they had no knowledge of our existence.

On Saturday, 19 January, an American voice gave out the news that a clash had taken place with Iraqi forces operating from the Kuwaiti oil platforms of the northern Gulf. Resistance had been quickly neutralised and twelve prisoners taken, stated to be the first prisoners of the war. Rubbish – what about our prisoner two weeks earlier? Two days later, the same reporter stated that Iraqi television had shown captured Allied airmen who looked as if they had been badly beaten. They made statements – which were highly suspect – that torture and coercion had been used. By this time the Coalition air force had flown over eight thousand sorties. They claimed that four out of five missions were reaching their targets, but bad weather had made accurate on-target assessments difficult. The main aim of the missions had been to eliminate Iraq's nuclear and chemical capability.

A weather report for the area followed: cold, followed by more cold. The Arab coats we had received on the last re-supply were good, but they were very heavy and prone to hold moisture, making them a double-edged weapon. The cracks in my hands were now getting so bad that if I didn't do something about them I knew I was in for serious trouble. The gloves we had been issued were next to useless, so I ended up using my socks as mittens. During the Falklands War cold had also been a problem, but within three weeks the SAS operating in the hides were issued with good Gore-tex clothing and gloves. This had been achieved by robbing the civilian camping stores of their stock. Three weeks into the Gulf campaign Arctic warfare clothing finally arrived from Hereford.

Our intelligence were certainly useless on weather conditions, but when it came to assessing the Iraqi military they seemed to be better. The Iraqi air force was not willing to fight, as most of its pilots were badly trained in combat situations. As it turned out, most Iraqi pilots flew their aircraft to Iran for the duration of the war. In fairness to the Iraqi combat engineers, from what we had seen of the defensive fortifications they were highly skilled; but Iraqi ground soldiers in defence were mostly conscripts and therefore not a problem. The real problem lay with Iraqi missiles and what they could deliver. Those Iraqi pilots who did fly aimed their attacks at Israel, backing up the Scud offensive, in the vain hope that Israel would enter the fray and upset the Coalition. But they were no match for the Israelis. Iraq had just taken delivery of about twenty Soviet long-range bombers. These Sukhoi-24s, used properly, would have posed a greater threat than the Scud-B missiles. They were equipped with the latest ground-hugging radar, and capable of delivering seven tons of high explosive with pinpoint accuracy. The problem was that the Sukhoi-24 required pilots of a very high calibre and a lot of bottle. Since both these elements were lacking, Iraqi attacks on Israel had to be carried out by the Scuds.

During the first two days of the war Iraq fired about fifty Scuds. So far none had carried a chemical warhead, but the threat of chemical or even nuclear delivery was very real. After the first salvo, American Patriot anti-missiles were hastily sent from the United States and positioned in both Israel and Saudi Arabia. They destroyed most of the Scuds in the air, but six got through to hit the cities of Tel Aviv and Haifa, and at least one struck Riyadh. Four Israelis and one Saudi died during these raids and at least 130 Israelis and thirty Saudis were injured, with more than a thousand Israelis being made homeless. However, just as the Israelis were about to attack the Iraqis, which would have upset the whole apple cart, their senior military people were told of our existence. Apparently, when General Schwarzkopf briefed the Israelis he informed them that he had put special forces deep behind the lines to counter the Scud threat. With some scepticism the Israelis asked, 'Whose special forces?' When Schwarzkopf replied, 'British SAS,' it is reported that the Israelis looked in disbelief and simply said, 'Brilliant.'

Any weapons expert will point out the deficiencies of the Scud missile and will tell you it's crap. It is very inaccurate – a dinosaur compared with the American Tomahawk cruise missile. The 37-foot-long missile traces its ancestry to the 1940s' V-2 rocket, which with the same degree of inaccuracy fell on London during World War II. As a Soviet client, Baghdad took deliveries of the ballistic missile and improved on its range, extending the Scud-B's maximum range of 280 kilometres to 620 kilometres. They did this, I am led to believe, by cutting the fuel tank in half and welding in an extra section. Many of these Heath Robinson-adapted missiles simply fell apart in the sky and never reached their targets. Still, the new improved Scud could pack 300 kilos of conventional explosives into a warhead. The problems would come if the missile was used to deliver chemical weapons.

No one outside Iraq knew for certain how many Scuds Saddam Hussein had in his arsenal before war broke out. Estimates ran at between five hundred and eight hundred. Baghdad possessed as many as thirty-two fixed launchers in silos and at least thirty-six mobile mounted units transported on huge eight-wheel trucks. The Coalition air force had managed to destroy most of the fixed launchers during the first air attacks, but more than half the mobile Scuds had survived. So who did they send into western Iraq, or 'Scud Alley' as it became known, to locate and destroy the mobile missiles? The SAS. It takes about five hours to prepare a Scud for use, and during this time we had to hunt the bastards down. But the country was very desolate. Watching main roads – the MSRs – was one way, but the Iraqi missile crews were very good. Looking at night for tell-tale signs of rocket exhaust was another means of detecting them, but you had to catch them setting up – once they had fired the missiles were long gone. To be honest, our half-column had very little luck actually catching the mobile launchers, although we tried bloody hard.

Now that we had made contact with the enemy, everyone seemed to settle down into a steady routine. Although problems with the leadership were soon to emerge, at first our half-squadron fighting column worked extremely well. We devised new tactics and deployments to outwit the enemy. As there were not enough night-vision goggles for every man, priority was given to the vehicle drivers, especially those in the lead wagons. We normally kept the column spread out; this tactic offered plenty of warning should the Iraqis suddenly appear. In such a situation the column would have time to line up broadside on, allowing all the guns to bear down. If for any

reason our long-range night-vision aids indicated enemy movement, or we were unhappy about crossing a particular stretch of
ground, the normal procedure was to stop and switch off the
engines. The bikes or one of the wagons would then go forward
and carry out a recce. There was very little talk during our
movement, and only on the rarest of occasions did we use the
radios – and then only to send a situation report or call for an
air strike.

The previous day we had identified an Iraqi military position
and sent back a report requesting an air strike. The response
was not as swift as might be thought, mainly due to the
availability of aircraft and the amount of air traffic flying at
any one time. In order to prevent hitting our own forces, the
system for target identification was highly complex. Most of
this work was done abroad the AWACs which flew continually
overhead. If the target was stationary there was not really a
problem, but if it happened to be a mobile Scud it would be long
gone before any Coalition aircraft arrived on the scene. However, on this occasion the head-shed did act and some time after
our report we saw the target being attacked by American A-10s.
Despite the vast amount of weaponry that the column carried, it
was always a comforting thought to know that we had air
power on call should we need it.

The one good thing about working behind enemy lines is the
lack of time for just sitting and thinking. We were constantly on
the move looking for Iraqi targets. We now found ourselves in
an area of Iraq that looked more like the surface of the moon
than part of the earth. The surrounding landscape had been
formed by the abrasive action of wind-blown sand, which over
the years had eaten at the rocks to form a series of small, saw-
toothed ridges interlaced with long, shallow, gully-type depres-
sions.

I sat on sentry duty, looking out over this desolate land and
waiting for darkness to fall. For once the weather had been

good, but now the sun had began to disappear behind the distant horizon and the cold was biting into my body. The thought that I might get killed here raised its head, as I am sure it did with every other soldier in the SAS. I was afraid, but the day you are not afraid is the day to leave. Many of the guys wrote special letters which, in the event of their death, would be sent to their next of kin. I did not do so myself: my boys know how much I love them, and if anything happened to me I know they would always remember me. Apart from that, I thought it was tempting fate. My main concern was to apply myself to the situation as best I could, and when the time came to fight I wanted to give a good account of myself. So I took good care of my physical condition, and despite the cold which was to play havoc with my hands, throughout the campaign I did not encumber any other member of our unit or stretch the meagre resources available to us.

A final ray of sunlight broke through the darkening sky and lit a path along which we would travel later that night. Brian had ordered Pat and me, together with three other wagons, to carry out a recce on an Iraqi radar installation. He and his faithful companion Mel had gone off with the rest of the guys to locate another target, an Iraqi airfield. I never thought splitting our group was a very good idea since it halved our fire-power.

Around midnight we found our target. We stood and observed the enemy from about one kilometre away before circling the target for a better view. That's when we came across a fibre-optic cable. This was good news. One of the best tasks in the whole war was blowing up fibre-optic communications cables. We knew the Iraqis were using fibre-optics, but they were normally buried several metres below the ground. At the very start of the Gulf War an SBS patrol, commanded by an SAS officer, had been ordered to collect a length of this cable for intelligence purposes. This raid was carried out some weeks before we went into Iraq. Two Chinook helicopters flew to a site less than 60 kilometres from Baghdad. When they got there both choppers landed on the main Basra road. While they waited, with engines running, the SBS dug up a 20-metre section of fibre-optic cable and left behind several explosive devices which destroyed even more of it. The raiding party took off and returned successfully to Saudi Arabia. One of the soldiers had stolen a ground marking sign which had indicated the cable, and this was presented to Norman Schwarzkopf. He was so delighted with the success of the mission that he relayed the news directly to Washington. This early operation was one of the key factors that persuaded the American commander to allow the SAS to operate in Iraq.

Although we could not see these cables, their position was easy to establish by the ground markers or manhole covers through which maintenance men got access. The latter were easy to spot, but most were alarmed. If we had tried to open them, the alarm would have alerted the Iraqis who would have come out in force. We dealt with the alarm by placing a large amount of explosive and several gallons of petrol on top of each inspection well. As any demolition man will tell you, a gallon of petrol, when detonated, will explode with the blast force of 7 lb of plastic explosive. In the case of the fibre-optic manhole it destroyed not only the cable but also any warning device.

If it was not appropriate to blow up the cable because the enemy were close by, we used another improvised method. First we would dig down and locate the cable. Then we would fix a tow chain between it and one of our vehicles, charge forward and uproot several metres. It was then just a matter of cutting out a section. This may sound primitive but the result was the same: total confusion to the Iraqi communications.

On this particular night, after destroying the cable we thought it best to get clear of the area in case the Iraqis sent out a patrol. Not that we were really too bothered about the

Iraqi forces: if they came too close we would give them a warm reception. One of the other half-fighting columns had proved this point. They had exchanged fire with the Iraqis before leaving. The Iraqis had insisted on following, so the guys gave them a fire-power demonstration. They waited in ambush, with all eight wagons training their main weapons on the approaching Iraqis. At a range of 500 metres they opened fire: Milans, Mark 19s, GPMGs and .50s all contributed to the wall of fire that greeted the enemy. After a few moments the column turned and drove off, but again the Iraqis followed. Once more the column waited in ambush, until eventually the Iraqis learnt their lesson and kept their distance.

Unfortunately we had only four wagons, so discretion seemed the better part of valour. We had also run out of darkness, and Pat gave the order to stop and find a place to lie up for the day. The first thing we did was report 'all well' to RHQ, who in turn would pass the message to Brian just to make sure that everybody knew we were okay. After passing the following day without incident, we packed up and made our way to rejoin the others. It was essential to do so as a re-supply was expected, and without Pat as navigator the other four vehicles would have been completely lost.

I was in the lead wagon, but I took it easy as I drove off because the ground was very rough. I found it hard to concentrate on our course as I was more concerned about the ground conditions. Sure enough we hit trouble.

Suddenly, without warning, the vehicle started to slip to the left, and next second it was rolling down a steep bank. I remember curling my tongue against my palate and clamping my teeth together as the vehicle bounced and leaped into space. Somehow I managed to jump out of my seat and over the top of Pat. I landed with a thump, rolling over and finishing up on my back. The landing sent a brain-to-bowel vibration through my body, as if my balls had shot up into my skull. Then I got that sick gut feeling that one experiences directly after an accident.

In slow motion I watched the wagon roll completely over. Pat was still in his seat, gripping the front of the wagon. Fortunately, the .50 Browning was mounted in the high position at the back of the wagon which saved him and the two guys in the back from getting crushed.

In a whirl of dust, the wagon came to a halt. The two in the back were trapped because all the loose equipment spilled on top of them. One guy, Mitch, shouted that he was okay, but Gav said he was injured; as it turned out, several of his ribs had been broken. Instantly the other vehicles came up alongside and we started to clear the mess of fuel cans, camouflage netting and ammunition boxes from the top of Mitch and Gav.

Both Pat and I were badly shaken, but since we had no broken bones we set to and cleaned up the mess. Gav was our priority and the medics went to work on him immediately, but judging from the noise he was badly injured. We retrieved the wagon, which although damaged was still in a usable condition, as were the weapons, and continued on our way.

When we joined up with the others Pat received yet another bollocking from Brian – mainly for not joining up the night before. By this time Gav was in a lot of pain and it was decided that he should be taken out on the re-supply helicopter. I had hurt my back and Brian wanted me to go out as well, but I told him I was staying.

Our task eventually ended up as a simple search and destroy mission. The idea was that we should watch the MSRs during the day, in the hope that we would observe something worth attacking. Unfortunately we saw nothing: the Iraqis were quick to learn that going out in the daytime brought swift death from the Coalition fighters. So we started watching the MSRs at night; this didn't work either, as we had to sit on the road to observe anything. The only times when our group saw any

Scuds were during the recce for the operation when one had been fired from the camp site, or so we believed; and when Pat thought he saw one while observing through the MIRA. Neither sighting could be confirmed. The other SAS groups did have a couple of incidents involving Scuds.

One fighting column, consisting of the other half of A Squadron, were carrying out a demolition task at the side of an MSR. As they were busy placing their explosives, two Iraqi trucks carrying missiles drove straight past them. This would not have been a problem except that it was in the middle of the day. Recognition was instant. The Iraqis realised they were in for big trouble and accelerated in an effort to escape. The column commander instantly made the decision to go after them and take them out. What then ensued can only be likened to one of those Westerns in which Indians chase a train.

Our lads chased the fleeing Iraqis, the bikes racing ahead trying to cut them off. As we came within range, we started to engage. There was a lot of firing and in the end both Iraqi vehicles crashed into the ditch at the side of the road. Within seconds the pursuing SAS lined up to engage them with their heavier automatic weapons. Two guys, Shug and Colin, both on bikes, closed on the rear Iraqi truck. Shug dumped his bike and ran forward to engage the soldiers. Colin moved to cover Shug. They came under an incredible amount of fire as the enemy tried to make good their escape. Suddenly, Shug was hit and dropped to the ground. Desperate to help his friend, Colin ran forward to provide covering fire. As he reached Shug, the wounded man simply looked up and said, 'I've been hit.' With that he slumped over to one side and died.

The mayhem continued, with devastating fire being laid down by our lads and rockets exploding in the burning Iraqi trucks. Then, suddenly, Colin too was hit. The round took him in the side of his chest, but luckily he was wearing a protective vest. Although he was wounded, it saved his life.

It was three days after Shug's death before our half-squadron were informed. Even then, they did not say who had died. In the field we use a system which is called NAAFI numbers. Each soldier has a three-digit number for the whole operation, which is used in all messages so that individuals can be identified without giving away their names over the radio. Unfortunately, for security reasons Pat didn't bring out the NAAFI numbers for the other half of our troop. It was two weeks before we found out that it was Shug who had been killed. When Pat called all the troop guys to the back of our wagon and told us the news we were devastated. Mel came over and attempted to say something, but due to our loathing of the man we gave him the cold shoulder.

Mel was turning into a real arse-licker. He would come up alongside Brian's wagon and say, 'For fuck's sake, Brian, put me up front. I'll make some ground up quicker than this twat.' This was in reference to Pat, and Brian would normally agree with him. Slugger, who was on Brian's wagon, would tell us about it later, mimicking Mel's voice. At least we got a laugh out of it.

Sadly, of course, this sort of behaviour has a very detrimental effect on a group of men, normally forcing it into separate camps. Spending most of my time with Pat at the front of the column, I saw and heard a lot more than the guys at the back. If anything was happening, Brian would always confide in Mel first. If a recce was going out, then it was always Brian and Mel in one group, Pat and the rest in the other. Then one day Brian instructed Pat to take out a four-vehicle recce. No reason why – just do it. The target was an Iraqi microwave communications station.

'OK, fellas,' Pat told us. 'There's a microwave installation to the north of here, approximately 30 kilometres. Brian wants us to go there tonight and locate it, and find out as much as we can about it by doing a full CTR.' Pat looked at our faces. Obviously we wanted more information.

'What's the future intention, Pat?' someone asked.

'Not sure. Brian wouldn't say. But it looks like HQ may want us to take it down.'

'Does Brian know the future intentions?' I enquired, knowing full well that he did.

'Yes. But he's not ready to give us the full picture until after the recce report.'

'When do we go?' I asked.

'Tonight at last light. I'll give you all a briefing at 1630 hrs. All four of these wagons will be going.' With that Pat strode off, leaving us to talk among ourselves.

We had been driving for about two hours, and the going was difficult to begin with as the night was overcast. I tried to use PNG, but all I could see was dark green murk. It was hard to relate to ground features and keep the right direction. To help, Pat took over the navigation, constantly calling out for me to turn left or right. Eventually the cloud started to clear, and bright stars appeared against the dark canopy. I could make out the Plough and Cassiopeia; locating these two main constellations made it easy to pinpoint the Pole Star. That's one good thing about the Middle East: the stars are very clear and make astro-navigation much easier. Even with all the hi-tech navigational equipment at our disposal, simply looking at the stars keeps you on course and save stopping all the time.

Settling down, the recce group continued, driving steadily. Suddenly my PNG went white and blanked out – something very bright had appeared in front. In the sky was an extremely bright flare-type object which flew over our heads. Then I realised what it was: the Iraqis had just fired a Scud. It was just like watching a rocket take off from NASA. A bright booster rocket projected the missile into the sky, moving as if in slow motion. Our heads turned skywards, watching the rocket go into orbit and disappear amid the stars, heading in a slight westerly direction.

'Some poor bastards are going to get that on their heads in about twenty minutes' time,' Ian muttered.

He was right. It was heading towards Israel – almost certainly Tel Aviv. There was little we could do at that moment, other than take a fix on the launch site and report it later. The device had been fired from probably 20 kilometres away. There was one good thing, however: it told us that the Iraqis were unaware of our presence.

By the time we hit the highway we had been driving for some three and a half hours. The road was quite narrow, running high up on an embankment. Our target was the other side of this obstacle, and luckily for us there was a tunnel running under the road. Using the MIRA, we observed the MSR and the tunnel from a distance of 400 metres to confirm that both were clear. We discovered later that at one stage the Iraqis had taken to hiding their mobile Scuds under motorway bridges. We approached with caution.

Pat decided to take a closer look on foot, and took Ian and me with him. I stopped short to provide cover while they went into the tunnel and checked it out. It was so low that the only way to get the vehicles through was to remove the roll-bars.

'We can't do that – it's a pain in the arse. And anyway the weapons systems on them will then be useless to us,' objected Ian.

'Then we've got to go over it. Come on, let's get back to the others.' Pat had started walking back towards the vehicles when we were stopped by a noise to our rear and saw the lights of a vehicle heading up the road towards us and closing fast. By the time we had run the remaining 100 metres to our own vehicles the guys were in position behind the guns, ready to react. The enemy vehicle looked like a Land Cruiser-type pick-up. Through the MIRA we could make out a number of soldiers sitting in the back. For some reason it started to slow down as it came in line with us, and the first thing that rushed through my mind was that they had seen us. But then the vehicle picked up speed again and continued along the road, heading west. We moved off east to find a better route across the motorway. Within 500 metres the embankment faded out and the road sloped down to our level.

'Shit! They're coming back!' All heads in all four wagons turned at the same time. We instinctively turned our weapons, tracking the vehicle and ready to blow it off the face of the earth if required. But just as quickly they were gone once more. We deduced that the Iraqis were sending out clearance patrols, or more likely early warning for the Scud launchers. I moved up slowly towards the road, where I could see what looked like the square roof of a service station just like you would see on a British motorway. As we got closer, it became apparent that that's exactly what it was. The truth was, we could have been on the M1 in England. There was a service station across the road, petrol pumps and all. The only difference from the M1 was that this six-lane motorway had an irrigation ditch running along one side, which presented a problem. How were we to get the vehicles over? The ditch was about a metre wide and deep, making it impossible to drive across. But cross it we must, and that meant we would have to bridge it somehow.

We decided that two of the vehicles should drive down the motorway to see if there was an easier way. We took Mitch's vehicle and mine, while Richard and Jack remained with theirs to provide cover if needed. It was truly amazing. There we were, two SAS Land Rovers, all tooled up, lights out, driving down this great Iraqi motorway. After driving for about five kilometres we came across an interchange junction complete with flyover. I half expected to see graffiti scrolled all over the bridge wall. Since the ditch was still there Pat suggested we should just go back and bridge it there.

When we got there Jack said, 'We can see a big antenna and lots of buildings in the distance to the north.'

Pat had a look through the MIRA and confirmed, 'I think that's it, Yorky. That's the target. Have a look through this, will you?'

Looking through, I could see a large radio tower with microwave dishes all over it and a building at its base with a road in front of it, as well as lots of small buildings and vehicles round about. There was a great deal of movement in the area, with people walking around and vehicles moving along the roads. All of us agreed that it was a very large installation.

We got back on our vehicles and started moving away from the road. We were about 100 metres away when the enemy pick-up came back and pulled into the side of the motorway where we had just been. All the soldiers jumped off and started walking around their vehicle. I immediately pulled our wagon round so all the weapons systems could engage if necessary, and the other three did the same. We had no idea if the Iraqis had spotted us or not. They were reacting strangely, as if they knew that someone had been there but weren't sure who or why. We weren't worried; at this range we could shoot the shit out of these people, but of course if we did it would compromise our chances of attacking the microwave target. A Mexican stand-off continued for about five minutes, although it felt like thirty. Then the Iraqis mounted up and drove off. They would never know how close they came to getting wasted that night.

We arrived back at the LUP about one hour into daylight. Pat went and briefed Brian and Paul, the OC designate who had arrived on the second re-supply, while we got on with sorting out our wagons and equipment before getting our heads down. Pat was away no longer than ten minutes, and when he returned I could tell he was pissed off.

'That was quick, mate,' I said carefully.

'Yes. Brian's pissed off because he keeps getting woken up.

He was so restless and agitated he was hardly paying any attention to my report.'

'Well, I'm surprised at that. I thought he'd be wriggling around like a mad thing,' I said, grinning.

'Go on, then let's have your theory, Yorky!' Pat asked with a look of dread on his face. The other guys all turned to listen to my conjecture with bated breath.

'It's probably because Mel's stuck so far up his arse that he's a little bit agitated.' It brought a smile to a number of tired and dirty-looking faces. Pat looked at me, shook his head and walked round to his bergen. Thinking back, I really started something with that statement. From then on Mel became the butt of our crazy sense of humour – if you will excuse the pun.

Something strange was going on. There was a lot of activity around the two signallers, Chris and H, who were very busy on the radio. A long message seemed to be coming in, but Brian, who was standing guard as all messages arrived, read the signals and then hid them in his pocket. Whatever it was, Brian was not letting on for the moment. Some of the boys wondered whether we were to be withdrawn to Saudi, and there was even wilder speculation that the new orders would send us directly to Baghdad. Eventually word came around that we were to carry out an attack on a microwave installation. Confirming orders for the attack would come later that day at 1600 hrs. We spent most of the day preparing for the operation, which was to be carried out at night, even though we were still unsure of precisely what we should be doing. Despite Brian's secretiveness, Charlie and H were good troop signallers and kept us informed about what intelligence was being sent over the radio. They even told us that Brian had told them not to say anything to the rest of us. This caused obvious problems and added to our confusion. How were we to operate if we were not given full information? Brian ordered some of the mountain troop guys to make a model of the microwave installation and the immediate area. This is normal army procedure when planning an attack, and the SAS is no exception. The guys built a beautiful accurate scale model from various items of equipment; considering that all they had to work from was the intelligence coming over the radio, it was a pretty impressive job. However, much of the intelligence on enemy strengths and dispositions was confused.

At 1545 hrs we gathered at the centre of the LUP by the model. Obviously some guys had to stay on sentry duty; they would be briefed on the operation afterwards. This is not ideal because the sentries do not get a thorough briefing. Once orders have been issued everyone is too busy getting prepared for the job, and the sentries go into the operation not knowing what the hell is going on. Still, in our situation sentries were vital.

It was clear and sunny, with a crisp breeze, as we formed up around the model. I say formed up, because Mel was putting us in the order that Brian wanted us in. Doing this makes it very clear who is in which party. He placed the fire support group on the left and the assault and cover men on the right. After we had looked at the model Brian and Paul, the OC designate, came over and began to brief us. Paul was fattish and in his mid-thirties. Rumour had it that he had hardly excelled at selection, but due to the dire need for officers he had somehow slipped through. Although Paul was a major, Brian was still very much in charge. Funny old army!

'RHQ want us to destroy a radar installation known as Victor Two. It's the main control centre guiding the mobile Scud units to their targets. American Stealth bombers have made several attacks on the location, much of which is underground. As AWACs aircraft have continued to monitor communications being transmitted from the site, the decision has been taken to send us in. Even at this late stage the Iraqis might still force the Israelis into the war, seriously damaging the Coalition.'

Brian paused in case anyone wanted to ask a question. When none were forthcoming, he continued.

'We're going to drive to within 1500 metres of the objective and place the vehicles in a fire support position. At this stage a recce group will go forwards, confirm the location and return. The recce group will then tie in with the remainder of the assault team and close fire support before guiding us on target. On target we will form up and carry out our task, which is to totally destroy the building housing the equipment and the microwave dish. Once our mission is completed, we'll return to the vehicles and make our way back to this location.' Brian stopped for a second time. Still there was no interruption.

'Groupings – I'm the overall commander, and I'll be going in with the assault group. Assault group one will consist of Slugger, Ian and Yorky. Mel, Mitch and Alistair will make up assault group two. Paul, Gav and Matt are assault group three. Dev, Jack and Stu, you will go as close fire support and be ready to assist in making entry into the complex. The fire support group commander will be Pat, with Richard as second-in-command. Everybody else will be on the vehicles giving fire support and driving as required.'

Still no interruptions other than the nodding of heads and the odd glancing exchange between the guys.

'The objective consists of a building complex with a microwave tower at the base approximately 65 metres feet in height. There's an internal security fence approximately three metres high, with an outside perimeter wall standing at five metres. The main gate is covered by a sentry position. While the recce is taking place, I want the mortar set up on to the objective for covering the assault party. The close support group will fire two 94mm anti-tank missiles, one at the sentry position and one at the main gate. Slugger, you will place an explosive charge on the inner fence. When it goes off, all three assault teams will effect an entry into the building complex.' Although all the anti-personnel and bar mines were divided among the vehicles, Slugger and Ian would normally deal with any explosive task as they were both trained in advanced demolition.

'The building is one floor above ground level, with two further floors below the ground. The floors are connected by a central staircase, and each assault team will take one floor. Slugger, you and your team will go down to the bottom floor, where the main control centre is. Clear the area and lay your charges, then get the hell out of there. The other two assault teams will each take a floor, clearing them of Iraqis before placing their charges. Once this is done, get the hell out. Right? Now let's get to the finer details.'

Most of us already knew what our tasks would be, once we were on the objective. Brian and Mel had come over to my vehicle earlier in the day to look at the spyglass, because I was the only man in our group who knew how to use it. They were asking me about the device and its characteristics, and what use it would be on the recce. Since neither of them had a clue how it worked, it was obvious that I had to be on the recce. As for my position in the actual assault, Slugger had told me that I was to be his and Mitch's cover man as they entered the control room. I was pleased about this. Slugger was a sergeant and a thoroughly professional soldier who since our arrival in Iraq had spent a great deal of time trying to offer good advice. Unfortunately, Brian would not listen to him. After the war Slugger's career took a dive and a lot of the lads slagged him off, but they had not heard the expert advice he was constantly giving to Brian. Brian, of course, was too busy listening to his mate Mel.

Ignoring the internal politics, I had spent most of the afternoon preparing my equipment and working out what I would do during the assault. By the time we received our orders from Brian I knew broadly what was happening.

As Brian finished his briefing, he explained about the Iraqis at the installation. RHQ had told him that there were only a few military personnel and the rest civilians, so he reckoned there should be no real problems. I looked at Matt standing next to me and we both whispered, 'Bollocks.' If they couldn't make a direct hit on the installation, how could they assess who was actually manning the microwave station? I found it weird that people could say things like 'There should be no real problems.' We were in the middle of Iraq and at war, not a fucking tea party.

I could see the other guys looking around at each other after Brian's comment. He finished by saying, 'We have the upper hand on these bastards. Let's get in there, do the job and get out again.' Then he added, 'Remember, fellas, everybody that goes in comes out. We don't leave anybody in there, no matter what.' That wasn't the first time I had heard that said. With hindsight I think he was scared shitless of being left behind.

Then he turned to Paul, the OC designate, asking if he would like to say a few words. To our total disbelief he said he would.

He was a typical officer – I know fucking everything – casting his chosen words over his men. 'Okay, men, let's not be under any illusions. This is a difficult job, but we can do it. We are better than them, better equipped than them and, like Brian said, we have the drop on them. Remember, also, that you will write yourselves into the history books as members of the first, and probably only, squadron attack of the Gulf War. You can feel proud of yourselves for that fact. But, gentlemen, remember there are a lot of people on that position, most of them innocent civilians. I don't want any indiscriminate shooting. Make sure you identify your target as enemy soldiers.'

Here we go again! Who the fuck do they think they are kidding? There we were, 400 kilometres behind enemy lines; to us everybody was an enemy. At night, when you can't see who's who, you have to assume everybody is the enemy. This doesn't mean you go around shooting at shadows, but it's a case of them or us. I could see by looking at the guys that there was more than an element of doubt in all their minds. So as soon as Paul had finished and Brian asked if there were any questions, we all raised the same point about indiscriminate shooting. But neither Brian nor Paul would back down; we had to treat everybody as civilians unless identified to the contrary.

The briefing was over. As I walked back to the wagon, Matt fell in step beside me. 'Well, Yorky, I guess RHQ is wanting to blood the troops.'

This was the first time I had heard this expression, 'Sorry, Matt – say again?'

'It's a term we used in the Falklands whenever the hierarchy wanted their young guys to go into battle, to give them the experience of war.'

'So what you're saying, Matt, is that this attack is irrelevant, yes? All this is just so the regiment can say one of its squadrons made an attack during the Gulf War?'

'That's exactly what I'm saying. And I'll stick my neck out further and say the regiment knows exactly how many troops are on that location, and whether they're soldiers or civilians. Hence my term, "blooding the troops".'

He had a point. How could RHQ have so much information on the objective, especially the building, but so little about enemy strengths and dispositions? An element of doubt bugged a lot of the guys that afternoon, and it was to prove a major problem later that night.

When I had made my final preparations, I joined Pat, Matt, Mark, Mitch, Ian and Slugger at the back of my wagon and we all stood around swilling a big mug of tea each. It would be the last brew for a while, but Pat had performed his regular chore of filling his big Nissan thermos flask with hot chocolate. It was a ritual he went through almost every night. When patrolling during the early hours of the morning, it wasn't possible or tactical to stop and brew up. Looking at the guys standing there, each with a mug in his hand, somehow epitomised the SAS in the Gulf War. I got one of the guys to take a photo of Ian and me in our full fighting kit, ready to go on the operation. 'Good luck, mate.'

'Cheers, Yorky.' We shook hands.

Then, climbing into our vehicles, we formed up in our order of march. As usual my wagon was at the front, with Pat navigating and me driving. At 1830 hrs we moved out, by which time it was getting colder as the darkness closed in, but there was still about forty-five minutes of light left. The column headed north towards Victor Two.

After driving for about two and a half hours we got our first sight of the MSR. I stopped the wagon and waited for the Land Rover fitted with the MIRA to come alongside. This would give us a better view of the MSR. Checking for activity, we half expected an Iraqi patrol to pass by, as they had last night. We had been observing for ten minutes or so when Brian drove up.

'What the fuck is happening?' He was not in a good mood.

'Just checking it's all clear,' replied Pat. 'Well, is it?' snapped Brian.

'Yes,' stated Pat in a tone that implied we were only doing our job.

'Well, let's get a fucking move on.'

'What an arsehole,' I thought. But then he was in charge. We moved off again and drove to the area which we had occupied the night before. Again we stopped. From here on we would need to deploy tactically. My vehicle, together with Mitch's and Jack's wagons, went forward to bridge the gap at the side of the road. We went past the service station and located the best position to form a vehicle bridge. I drove my wagon to within 30 centimetres of the ditch, facing head on. All the mobility troop guys were there ready to assist. After measuring the distance between the wheels, we placed four sandbags on either side in the ditch before bridging the gap with two sand channels. Bridging the ditch in this way allowed us to drive the wagons over the gap without them getting grounded – if one got stuck it would be a hell of a problem to get it out.

To see if it would work I jumped back on my wagon, started her up, selected low ratio first gear and moved forward. Slowly dropping the front wheels on to the sand channels supported by the sandbags, I inched my way across. Slugger and Alistair stood watching either side of the wagon, with Pat at the front. All of them indicated that I was okay and that the bridge was holding. When my front wheels touched the far side of the ditch I applied more revs to the engine and powered the wagon up the rise in front of me. I was over.

Dealing with the ditch hadn't been a real problem to mobility troop; we were always doing such things in training and it had become second nature. It had taken less than two minutes to lay the sandbags and get my wagon across. But we had to press on, as it was going to take some time to get the others over too. It took seventeen minutes to complete the task. There was no enemy movement, and it all went like clockwork.

As usual mobility troop were left to clear the equipment away. We carried the sandbags back to our wagons so as not to compromise the operation by leaving evidence of our presence for the enemy to find. Mounting up once more, we moved off towards Victor Two.

When we were about five kilometres from the objective, the tension started to rise. It's something that grips you inside – a heightened awareness of everything around you. As we moved forward we expected the Iraqis to spring an ambush, or that we would simply run into a large enemy force. You project your senses into the darkness, watching for the slightest sign or movement; your body somehow stretches, ready for that burst of immediate action.

Suddenly the ground we were crossing became very difficult, causing us to deviate from our intended route. This detour took us about a kilometre to the west, where the ground was a mass of man-made slit trenches, all cut in long lines. Although this posed a problem, my orders were to stop or slow down only if I saw any enemy vehicle movement. As we approached the objective, the MIRA wagon came forward and to our left. It was vital that we continually observed the area as we got closer.

'Stop.' It was Pat's voice, 'We're about 1500 metres away now. I think this is where we should hold.'

It had been arranged that at the 1500-metre point Alistair would leave his bike, which would be logged into the Satnav so as to give us a position to make our way back to after the operation. As this was being done, Brian came alongside in his wagon. 'What's wrong now?'

'Nothing. We're 1.5 kilometres from the objective,' said Pat, his eye still stuck to the MIRA.

'What can you see?'

'Not too sure yet. Give me a chance!' While Pat used the MIRA to check the position I got the spyglass out and did the same. The location was massive. There were lots of vehicles, buildings and people all milling around the objective. I could make out soldiers sitting in slit-trenches, as well as several bunkers; people were moving between all these locations. It was clear that most of them were carrying weapons.

I turned to Pat. 'So much for all the Iraqis being civilians.'

I was about to elaborate when Brian cut in. 'Fuck it. Let's get closer.'

So off we drove once more, making nonsense of the initial plan. As we closed on Victor Two, Pat murmured, 'At this rate, Yorky, we're going to end up with every wagon in the middle of the position.'

I was about to reply when two wagons pulled past me on my left. 'What the fuck's happening?'

'Mel's taking the lead with the MIRA,' Brian shouted out.

'Fucking surprise, surprise,' Pat replied. We get the column to the target, then they take over to be first on the objective.'

We continued driving towards the buildings, which by now were quite visible against the skyline. The next thing I noticed was that we were on a tarmac road running directly into the camp. On either side of us were dozens of vehicles and Iraqi soldiers. No one except Brian and Mel had a clue about what was happening. Pat wanted to stop and brief the others, but he couldn't risk losing contact with Mel and Brian, who had driven off with the MIRA. Then we were driving straight through the enemy position: eight vehicles in a line, just driving past the enemy slit trenches, their vehicles and buildings as if it was a Sunday afternoon stroll.

Somehow I became relegated to fourth vehicle in column, without knowing how I had got there or what was going on. There's an old saying that orders only survive the first round fired in battle. Our orders had already changed beyond recognition, and we hadn't fired a single shot yet.

Suddenly, without warning, we were stopping, pulling over to the left side of the road. The wagons formed up in line alongside a small escarpment that ran parallel to the road. It was dark and cold but I didn't notice the temperature – the adrenaline was keeping me warm. I could clearly make out the target area.

Pat whispered to me, 'I'm not too sure what's going to happen from here on.' .

'I'll get my spyglass, because we've got to do some sort of CTR. Why don't you go and speak to Brian? Tell him we don't have a fucking crystal ball back here.'

Pat went off towards Brian's vehicle. The whole episode was becoming quite theatrical. There we were, in the middle of a huge enemy position, trying to make up our minds what we should do next. Some of the guys stayed on their vehicles, while others stood around whispering to each other. It was more like an exercise than a wartime operation.

Pat came back. 'Okay Yorky, as planned, you're going forward on a CTR with Brian, Mel, Slugger and me.'

'Okay, no problems.' I replied.

Pat quickly briefed a couple of the other guys and left them to provide all-round defence. He also told them to be ready to move once the recce party returned. As Pat and I joined Brian and the others, it became obvious that Brian was anxious to get started.

'Let's go,' he said. 'Yorky, up front. Lead scout.'

We moved off. Our close target recce discovered how big the location really was. In all, it stretched almost a kilometre square, with the vast tower covered with communications dishes and control buildings dominating its centre.

The trouble with our original plan was that it had been devised by our RSM, Brian. At best it had a tendency to be what one might call 'flexible'. To put it in plain English, no one had a fucking clue what was happening. We simply survived minute by minute. Having driven straight into the camp and parked behind a large sand bank, there was little else to do but carry on. It was some 300 metres from the vehicles to the main communications complex, which I could now make out. The tower and the immediate control buildings were surrounded by a wall, inside of which, although we couldn't see it, was a second perimeter fence. The Stealth bombers had seriously damaged the buildings on the surface, but the tower was still up and the place was defiantly operational.

I remember trying to ask Brian a number of questions at that point, just to clarify his intentions in my mind. I wanted to know what route we were taking, what actions we should take on contact, and so on.

'Look, we've got no fucking time for that shit. Let's go.' This was Brian's answer to everything. If he didn't have an answer he'd simply tell you to fuck off. I decided to make the best of a bad situation – at least I could rely on men like Pat and Slugger.

The point of having a lead scout is to give an early warning to the rest of the patrol. This allows them to gain some advantage over the enemy, or, as we say, 'get the drop on them'. It is the most dangerous position within the patrol. More often than not, during any contact the lead scout is first to be either wounded or killed.

As I moved forward silently, everything around me appeared very quiet and still. The night air was cold, the sky very clear and dusted with bright stars which shone a great deal of light over the position. Suddenly the ground to my front opened up, allowing me to see more of the surrounding area. To my left the burne line continued to run in the direction of the target. Directly to my front I could make out some small buildings, while to the right there was a larger, square building. I could also distinguish the road that ran parallel to the burne about 50 metres to my right. We would need to move out into the open and cross that road in order to reach the target.

We stopped and everyone got down in all-round defence, except Brian who stood and surveyed the area. Then he simply said, 'Okay, I've seen enough. Let's get back to the others and get this fucking job done.'

Our CTR was as brief as that. We returned, retracing our steps alongside the burne. Gathering us together, Brian quickly went over a revised plan. It was quite simple: the vehicles would split into two groups and give cover from the flanks. While the main group, comprising the demolition teams and a cover party, went in on foot to carry out the demolition job on the tower, the main fire support group of five wagons would follow the burne until they were almost parallel to the target. The second group of three wagons would stop more or less where we had terminated our CTR.

We formed up in our groups and set off. Once more I was delegated as lead scout. We quickly moved forward, using the same route we had taken for the CTR. I had moved about 20 metres from this point when I made an observation check with the spyglass. I stopped, holding up my left hand to indicate a halt to the rest of the patrol. Dropping down on one knee to reduce my silhouette, I swept the area. The position was far larger than I had expected, and there was a great deal of activity over to the right. There were five lines of tents, making approximately fifty tents in total. Although there was no movement, the thermal imager definitely registered heat coming from inside. Given the time of night, the soldiers must be sleeping. Then I detected movement just to my right. One man moving. No – two . . . three . . . five men, and they were all carrying weapons. I counted some twenty soldiers in all.

'Hang on,' I said to myself. 'They can't be soldiers – they're supposed to be civvies.' I turned around to speak to Brian, who was behind me acting as my cover man. I couldn't believe it; he was standing there facing the burne, with his left hand in his pocket and his right hand gripping the barrel of his M16 which slung on his shoulder. Behind him were three guys on their knees covering different directions – left, right and rear. But not Brian. I clicked my tongue to alert him to come closer.

'What the fuck's wrong?' His northern accent made him sound as if he didn't give a damn.

I quickly explained the situation. 'Look, cut the fucking shit and get us to the target,' Brian replied.

'It's not in view yet.'

'Well, let's get fucking going, then.'

He never ceased to amaze me. I stood up and moved cautiously forward once more, but I felt far from confident with Brian as my cover man. After a short distance I noticed a dark patch – a long oblong shape on the ground to my front. The thermal imager showed it to be a trench, but I was not sure if it was occupied or not. I stopped once more and dropped to my knees, giving the thumbs down sign. Brian appeared by my side, standing as usual.

'What the fuck is it now?'

'Slit trench, 20 metres to our front.'

'Any fucker in it?'

'Can't see!'

Without waiting for me to check with the imager Brian walked forward and kicked a large sheet of corrugated tin which had been half covering the trench. The noise of clanking metal filled the air and I was sure that someone would hear. Returning to where I was kneeling he said, 'Come on, there's no fucker there. Let's get going.'

Now either this guy was Mr Cool, or he was too stupid to be true. I even began to question myself. Was it me? Was I doing this all wrong? I continued checking with the imager until I noticed a gap in the burne line. Immediately I went down on one knee, bringing the spyglass up to my eye. I could sense Brian standing behind me.

'What the fuck's up now?' he snapped. His voice was so loud that I thought the Iraqis were going to hear him.

'You stupid prick,' I said silently, then made a 'shushing' sound in the hope that Brian would get the hint and shut the fuck up. Through the TI I could make out the corner of a sandbagged bunker concealed by the edge of the burne. I could not see if there was anybody in the position.

Brian demanded again, 'Is there anybody in there?'

At this point I was close to losing my temper. 'For fuck's sake, Brian, there's a bunker just by the burne. I can't see into it.'

At that, he just walked over to the bunker and jumped in with no thought of the consequences. Luckily for us there wasn't anybody in there.

'There's nobody in there!' he informed me on his return.

'I think that's quite fucking obvious,' I replied tersely. By this time I had had enough and told him that I was moving off in the direction of the burne line. I was furious at the way he was casually walking behind me with his weapon tucked under his arm.

We patrolled another couple of hundred metres before we saw the target. This was our first sight of the position that we had come to destroy. Once more I started to observe with the spyglass, noticing that there was a large black sheet draped over the entry position. I informed Brian but he wasn't interested and merely told me to get a move on. Then I heard the sound of a large vehicle and at the same time the view in my spyglass blacked out. To my complete surprise there was a bus heading directly towards us. I immediately dropped to the ground, taking cover behind a small sand bank. Turning, I noticed all the others diving for cover too. Brian just stood there and said, 'You're a windy bastard! Right, you and Slugger get back to the rest of the group and tell them to bring the vehicles up here.'

As Slugger and I set off I said, 'That lunatic is going to get us fucking killed.'

Slugger agreed, 'Yes, I know, mate. We're just going to have to be very careful – get the job done and then get the fuck out of here as quickly as possible.'

We quickly briefed the guys, then returned to where Brian was waiting. He was surrounded by a whole group of men: one burst of enemy fire would have taken most of them out. What the hell was going on? It turned out that he had got all the assault team together and was giving them a bollocking. We stood there in total amazement. He then proceeded to give us another change of plan. The problem was that not everybody was totally aware of the changes, and this proved to be very dangerous.

I was now ordered to go with Paul, acting as the cover party. There was a truck parked to the right of the target which would serve as our position. It proved to be a fuel tanker with bowser attached to the rear. When Paul and I arrived, everything seemed peaceful. As we watched the demolition party move off towards the target, our luck seemed to be holding and my feeling of apprehension disappeared. Suddenly I was feeling excited.

I recall noticing that the fire support group were not yet in position, and thought that we should therefore not attack the target yet although by this stage I wasn't sure whether their orders had been changed.

As the assault group closed on the target I moved round the truck, dropping to one knee near the bowser. Paul knelt alongside me. It was deathly quiet. I watched the remainder of the assault group move alongside the perimeter wall, covering them as they disappeared beneath the black tarpaulin sheet that served as a doorway. They had been gone for just a few seconds when suddenly I heard a noise from the truck. Paul heard it too and looked questioningly at me.

Very quietly he whispered, 'What the fuck was that?'

I moved slowly forwards, heading towards the cab. More movement, and definitely a mumbling noise. 'Shit. There's someone in there!'

Paul put his hand on the lever and tried to open the door. It would open only a fraction, and then we realised that it was tied with a piece of string. Paul moved away from the door and I stepped forwards and grabbed it, pulling hard so that the string broke. The door burst open to reveal a boy who, although in uniform, could have been no older than sixteen. In the brightness of the starlight I could see the whites of his eyes, his cheeks and short dark hair. My brain took a mental snapshot of him. In the same instant I pushed my rifle into the boy's chest, shaking my head in an attempt to indicate that he should keep quiet. Then I realised that there was another man in the cab.

The boy started to move backwards, pushing himself deeper into the seat. His voice was squealing in Arabic, 'No. No. No!' I had one last try at keeping him quiet, but the boy was scared shitless. Then he made a move for his rifle, which lay beneath him. We moved in unison: his hand gripped the stock of his rifle as I pushed my rifle hard into his chest. We both knew what was going to happen next. Our eyes locked, and he registered my decision to kill him. For a split second everything around me disappeared. I could not see or hear anything except this young boy. Then I pulled the trigger and blew him away. Even as the bullets ripped into his chest his head was shaking and pleading. But it was all in vain.

As my two rounds punched hard through his chest at point blank range a burst of rapid fire flew over my shoulder into the cab. Paul had opened fire. Instinctively I peeled away to the left, realising after firing my second round that my weapon had a stoppage. The noise from Paul's automatic rifle was unbelievable as the rounds ripped through the bodies of the two Iraqis and the opposite cab door. Instantly enemy fire started coming from every direction. Several Russian-made SU22 anti-aircraft guns added their contribution. By comparison our weapons seemed puny, and even the Milans failed to be heard; nevertheless we laid it down thick and heavy. There was no point in being quiet any more, since we were now well compromised. Luckily at this point none of the fire was very effective, but the volume was tremendous. Red and green tracer rounds buzzed around like little hornets, ricocheting off the ground and deflecting in every direction. But from the direction of the incoming fire it was obvious that the enemy didn't have a clue where we were.

Realising that the demolition party would be coming out through the wall at any moment, I ran to the back of the truck and shouted for Paul to follow. The first thing I saw was two of our guys taking up position slightly forward of another truck just left of the target. Next moment a figure jumped out of a truck on to one of the guys. I found out later that it was my best mate Des, who had been ambushed by an Iraqi soldier. Like the two whom Paul and I had shot, he had been asleep in the cab. The pair of them struggled for a moment, then the Iraqi broke free and ran like hell towards the burne line. I took a bead with my rifle on the running man, but he was crossing open ground with the fire support group immediately behind him. I could see no weapon, and was unsure if he was a soldier or a civilian. I held my fire and the man disappeared into the dark.

Inside the target compound, the demolition teams quickly fitted the charges. Stealth bombers had already done a good job and inflicted severe damage on the control centre. Our guys had just finished fitting the charges to all four legs of the microwave tower when the noise of small arms fire alerted them. On Slugger's command the four men fired off their grip switches, timing the explosive to detonate in one minute and thirty seconds. Then the assault team prepared to leave. Ben led them out, covered by Alistair. Quickly they checked the entrance area. Although there were no Iraqis in sight the tracer rounds were zipping by, blocking their exit. If they tried to make a break for it, the enemy would cut them down. On the other hand, in just over a minute there was going to be one hell of an explosion and the huge tower would come crashing down on top of them. With no alternative the assault group burst out, running like mad for cover. Luckily no one was hit.

I watched as the guys ran from the entrance point, rapidly heading back towards the burne and the protection of the support wagons. It was time for Paul and me to join them. We both ran, ducking and weaving towards the vehicles. As we approached them I yelled out, 'Yorky and Paul coming in from the left,' just to make sure they knew who it was. As we dived in behind the nearest wagon, a massive explosion ripped through the air. Although we had all been expecting it, the shock wave blast felt like a tornado. Three of the four demolition charges had gone off on time, and the large tower slowly buckled to one side and collapsed. The grating sound of metal on metal rose out of the dust.

The explosion caused the enemy fire to become more intense,

but it was still not very effective. Not wanting to wait for the Iraqis to get their act together, we quickly slotted into our exit formation. I was near the front and recognised Brian, Ian, Slugger and Matt all in front of me. We were just approaching our three wagons when I noticed several silhouettes moving on top of the burne.

'Who the fuck's that lot on the burne?' someone else asked.

'It's okay, they're civvies.'

Wrong. The silhouettes opened fire on us. Slugger dropped to the floor as the vortex of a high velocity round passed through his trouser leg. His immediate reaction was that he had been hit, but luckily the round itself never touched him. By this time Matt, Ian and I had reached the side of the Mark 9 wagon and quickly put the vehicle between the enemy and ourselves. To my left the roar of an engine made me notice that one of our wagons was taking off. However, at that moment I had other things on my mind.

Matt and Ian stood by the truck tailgate and poured some fire down on the enemy. I jumped up on the wagon and shouted for Leslie, who was sitting behind the Mark 19, to fire, indicating with my hand the direction of the enemy. But Leslie just grabbed the weapon and fired blindly into space, totally in the wrong direction.

'Fucking idiot,' I grabbed hold of the weapon and turned it towards the enemy on the burne. 'There! There!' I screamed at him over the noise.

Eventually he got a grip and started to engage the enemy. The rounds that Leslie had originally fired, had gone off in the direction of our main fire support group. One of the guys later reported coming under fire from a number of what he thought were light mortars. I jumped off the truck and joined Matt and Ian at the rear, from where all three of us fired for all we were worth towards the enemy position. By this time the amount of incoming fire was quite intense, but we tried desperately to stand our ground. Looking to my left, I saw more of our lads putting fire down towards the enemy.

'Where's Brian?' I shouted.

'He's fucked off in a wagon.'

Then I recalled hearing one of our vehicles start up and drive off. As we came under fire Brian had dived on to the front of the nearest truck and screamed to the driver, 'Get the fuck out of here!' One or two other men had managed to jump on the back as it drove way into the darkness, leaving the rest of us behind.

There was an incredible amount of confusion at this stage. However, most of the guys were capable of taking control of the situation. When the enemy fire increased, and our main fire support group had still not re-appeared, it was generally decided to move our position. Frank, who was driving the Mark 19, slowly moved the wagon away from the burne. He had some bottle, driving directly into the line of enemy fire. I shall never know how he managed not to get hit. Nor was he the only hero. The two guys who were operating the MIRA, which was mounted high on the vehicle roll-bar, stood up in the wagon directing fire throughout the battle. With enemy fire ranging all around, these two stood their ground. One of them, Barry, took a direct hit on the Milan missile that was right next to his head. Battle really is a proving ground, and Victor Two was no exception.

The red and green hornets were everywhere, dancing in the amazing fireworks display that only war can create. The crack and thump of a thousand rounds whistled all around us. Tracer rounds flew past at incredible speed, then stopped suddenly as they hit a hard surface. I heard zip, zip, zip as hot lead buzzed my arms, my legs and my head.

Amid this chaos the fire support group were fighting desperately to extract themselves. At the time they were unaware of the real situation, thinking that some of us were still on the target. Communications had gone down just when we needed them most, which meant that neither group knew what the other was doing and had been engaging anything that looked as if it might be sheltering an Iraqi soldier. Permanent buildings, Portakabins and vehicles all littered the area, burning brightly if they had been set on fire.

Throughout all this there was still time to laugh. One of the guys, Charlie, said he had spotted an Iraqi having a shit just before the fire-fight started. He could clearly see the guy through the infra-red sight attached to the GPMG. He engaged him more out of fun than in any attempt to kill him, and later explained in great detail how he had shot short bursts after the retreating Iraqi while he was still trying to pull his trousers up. Another guy, Sam, had spotted an Iraqi firing from inside one of the Portakabins, and decided to take the whole building out with a 66mm rocket. He shouted at another guy to use his 66mm. After assembling the weapon the guy aimed it from a distance of no more than 30 metres and pressed the tit. The rocket screamed away but missed the Portakabin by some two metres. Everyone, including a number of Iraqis, watched in amazement as the rocket disappeared into the night.

We had started pulling back from the burne and gone about 200 metres when the enemy fire found us once more. The bullets buzzed around like flies homing in on a piece of meat. There was a great deal of confusion as we retreated. I remember about eight of us running at the side of the one remaining wagon. The other two had gone, although we didn't know where, and we were just following their last known direction. I remember hanging on to the side of the wagon for protection when all of a sudden a massive amount of incoming fire barely missed the top of it. I looked round at my old mate Des and shook my head; we both knew it was getting very dodgy.

Next thing I knew, Mel was next to me and saying, 'This is a load of fucking shit!'

I just looked at him and said, 'Well, you're one of the head-shed, Mel. You sort it out – it's what they pay you for! With this I jumped off the vehicle. There was no way I was going to listen to Mel mouth off.

It felt as if we had been running for ages, although in reality we had probably covered no more than a kilometre or so. We stopped abruptly, as one of the guys said he could see two vehicles to our front and was sure they were ours. As we got closer we discovered that it was Brian's gang, which included Paul and some four or five more. It was obvious that the other guys had been either driving or commanding their vehicles, when Brian had jumped aboard and ordered them 'to get the fuck out of here'.

We formed up in all-round defence, preparing the wagons for a quick getaway if necessary. I thought that one of the vehicle commanders might take control, but it didn't happen. There were a number of junior NCOs who could have taken control, but this would probably have caused even more problems. We started talking in whispers, checking on who had made it back and who was still missing. Brian must have thought we were talking about him, for next minute he shouted out, 'Shut the fuck up, all of you.' At this point he tried to make a command decision. 'Right, we're getting the fuck out of here!'

In unison some ten voices shouted back, 'What about the fire support group?'

'They can make their own fucking way back.'

'Bollocks. We're not leaving.' The majority decision was to wait for the rest of the guys. Brian tried to bully his authority on the rest, but by this time we had had enough. I thought back to his briefing and the declaration: 'We don't leave anybody behind.'

It was around this time that I thought we were not going to make it. If the Iraqis followed, most of us would be forced to go on foot. I started to prepare myself mentally for a spot of E and E (escape and evasion). When we were all together our fighting had strength; split, as we were, I was starting to feel vulnerable.

Suddenly Barry, who was still manning the MIRA, shouted out, 'I can see some vehicles coming towards us. I think they're ours! Yes, it's the fire support group.' Ben, who was riding the only bike during the Victor Two assault, shot off into the darkness to make contact and bring them safely in. This action was to win him a Military Medal after the war. Bru opened up on his radio, also trying to contact them. Finally he succeeded, relaying our position precisely. Then someone thought of what seemed to him a good idea, 'I'll switch on my infra-red firefly.' This is a small, torch-like object which emits a very strong blue flashing light and is used as a distress beacon. Nobody got the chance to stop him. As the strobe light went on it instantly attracted the enemy fire, and high velocity rounds started pouring into our position.

'Switch it off! Switch it off!' The guys screamed as we all dived for cover. He had only been doing his best, but to recall this young man fumbling about trying to turn the confounded thing off would bring a smile to my face for years to come. Two minutes later the fire support group drove up, all of them alive and kicking. But a single look told you they had fought one hell of a battle. Best of all, Pat was back. Thank goodness for someone with a cool head and clear thoughts.

As soon as he arrived Pat took control, ordering everyone to mount up and prepare to move. He turned to Dave on the MIRA and requested, 'Find me a way through this position.' Then, checking the original Satnav location where Alistair had left the bike, he pointed his arm in front. 'Find me a hole in that direction!'

'There are enemy slit trenches all over the place along that route,' shouted Dave.

'Bring all the guns to bear in that direction – we're going to punch a lane through.' With that the column moved forwards, our guns cutting down any resistance. The enemy were still firing to our rear but nothing much was coming our way, and even if it did nothing was going to stop us. For an hour we ran the gauntlet of Iraqi soldiers before disappearing once more into the empty darkness of the desert.

I don't recall much about the rest of that drive to our LUP – I was just happy we had made it. Once we had arrived, Paul came around to my wagon and asked, 'I need to know your confirmed kills. It's for the sit-rep back to RHQ.'

'Just the two in the truck,' I said, not really wanting to be reminded of the young Iraqi.

Paul immediately said, 'You're not trying to take the credit for those two that I killed, are you?'

'What?' I replied, somewhat startled.

'You know – those two that I killed when that Iraqi fired a pistol at me.'

'Boss, this is not a fucking competition, you know. That Iraqi tried to get his weapon, so I shot him. Then I had a stoppage and you got the other one. Will that make you happy?'

He didn't answer and just turned away. Funnily enough, he didn't ask anybody else. When the vehicle re-supply came in, Paul submitted his report. It read exactly as I thought it would; he didn't even mention that I was with him, but named someone else instead.

Once we had regrouped and found that everyone was okay, the shit started to fly. Pat really had a go at Brian, mainly for his incompetence. It was very obvious that Brian resented Pat. Here was a man who had done more for the safety of the squadron than anybody, especially while attacking Victor Two. Yet for all his work on the operation Pat didn't receive any award. On our return from the Gulf, his career took a dive.

After the raid on Victor Two we were ordered to rendezvous for a spectacular vehicle re-supply which the head-shed had planned. A column of ten three-ton trucks laden to the gunwales with equipment and vehicle spares was assembling. It was to penetrate deep into Iraq and rendezvous with both A and D Squadrons. Six armoured Land Rovers from B Squadron would be providing the security, riding shotgun over the column. The rigours of the desert had taken its toll on all our vehicles, and many were in desperate need of mechanical repair. A complete REME workshop was included in the column, along with technical experts for fixing the Magellans and radios. The column commander was a major, a cool and very calculating SAS veteran. As they assembled in the early hours of 10 February, he issued his orders. 'We stop for nothing. Anything we hit we take on, and incoming effective fire means you are actually being hit!'

One of the base guys who saw the column leave said it was an emotional moment. The guys were all dressed in their long locally purchased Arab winter coats, and the line of trucks with the vehicles riding shotgun looked more like something out of the Wild West than an episode in the 1990s Gulf War. They made it, reaching the rendezvous, some 150 kilometres inside Iraq, at 1600 hrs three days later.

While the mechanics got to work, the men from the fighting columns refuelled and rearmed. Then it was time to eat some fresh food – real meat, bread and fruit. Such basic provisions mean a lot to soldiers who have consumed nothing but boil-in-the-bag food for weeks. I was surprised to find at the vehicle re-supply area several Iraqi prisoners, who had been captured by one of the other fighting columns when attacking a small Iraqi position. Our guys had discovered several Portakabin-type buildings which the Iraqis were using, and with no other sign of the enemy for several kilometres they decided to take the position out.

Using dead ground to hide their approach the guys moved quietly up to the Portakabins, which sat on a slight rise. Once they had reached the doors and could hear the soldiers talking inside, they went into action. First they threw in a few grenades. Once these had exploded, they shot everything inside. Several of the enemy were killed instantly.

Unfortunately, the grenades had started a fire and our guys were forced to retreat. Two Iraqis made a run for it, but were swiftly taken out. Two others that were trapped by the flames eventually made it by crashing through the decaying building and emerging like balls of fire. Our guys put out the flames and took them both prisoner.

Immediately the medics went to work, not just on the burns but also on the bullet wound that one of them had received. The fighting column moved off, taking the prisoners with them. They remained with the SAS column for two weeks, at which time the main vehicle re-supply had been set-up. Unfortunately one of the Iraqis lost his leg due to gangrene setting in, but both were repatriated after the war. During their period of captivity at the vehicle re-supply they were kept blindfolded, sitting wrapped in spare camouflage nets to keep them warm. They were only young guys of seventeen or eighteen years old, and after a few days everyone was feeding them biscuits and sweets. It's a strange old world. Since the bulk of the regiment was in one location, albeit Iraq, Brian, in his capacity as RSM, decided to call a sergeants' mess meeting. At midday on 16 February some thirty-five senior NCOs convened in the centre of the re-supply area to discuss forthcoming functions and other mess business, one of which was voting funds to equip the mess with £30,000 worth of new leather furniture. The vote was carried, and in due course the mess purchased some of the finest furniture available. There is a wonderful photograph of this mess meeting, which later every member signed; the signatures include those of Norman Schwarzkopf and Peter de la Billiere. For the rest of us there was time to speak to members of the other fighting columns, hear what they had been doing and pick up on gossip. It was just one more of the many bizarre events of the war in the Gulf.

6

THE COST OF WAR

Our half-column was not the only one to have some fun in Iraq. Most of the other fighting columns and observation patrols had regular contacts with the enemy. One battle took place during the early hours of 9 February, just before the rendezvous with the re-supply, and news had arrived that Dave, the SSM (squadron sergeant major) of A Squadron, had been killed, although officially he was wounded, missing in action.

His team were carrying out a CTR on a communications installation, with Dave in command. They had moved on to the target in the dark hours, and the SSM was standing on the back of a wagon, observing through the MIRA. The team had already cut their way through the barbed wire which surrounded the installation, leaving one wagon at their entry point to act as cover.

Moving further into the Iraqi position, Dave realised that the place was far bigger than he had originally thought. However, by this time they were committed and there was no point in doing half a job. He told Andy, his driver, to keep going. Suddenly, as they topped a small rise, Dave made out some shadowy movement through the MIRA. Realising that there were enemy all around, and it was just a matter of seconds before contact would be initiated, he made a snap decision to bluff it out and drive through the Iraqi position as quietly as possible. They had not been seen yet, and the dark should conceal their identity.

'Good way to do a recce!' remarked Andy.

As they continued weaving their way through the Iraqi defences and accommodation buildings, a soldier stepped out in front of the wagon and made an attempt to stop it by holding up his hand. Terry, who was sitting in the front passenger seat manning the GPMG mounted in front of him, opened up with a large burst of 7.62mm. The soldier disintegrated, and then there was mayhem.

For some inexplicable reason, even though it was dark the wagon was targeted immediately by the Iraqis. Seconds later the three SAS guys were taking incoming fire from all directions. Dave was hit in the first burst. A round went through his upper leg, knocking him off balance and throwing him into the back of the wagon. At the same time Andy booted the vehicle forwards, accelerating hard and hoping to burst out.

At one stage it looked as if they were going to make it. Swerving and driving like a maniac, Andy drove straight through the camp gates while Terry blasted away with the GPMG. Then their luck ran out: 300 metres from the camp gates the wagon crashed into a large tank ditch. Seconds before, Dave had raised himself, hoping to get the rear gun into action. The sudden stop threw him forward over the roll-bar, where he landed half on the laps of Andy and Terry and half on the bonnet. His leg was lying across his chest.

Shaking themselves, they immediately made to escape. Andy threw Dave on his shoulders and started to run, trying to put distance between themselves and the wagon, which was now on the receiving end of the Iraqi fire. With Terry covering, they attempted to melt into the darkness.

Those who know the SSM would describe him as a large, well-built man, with a mental strength to match that of his body. But the damage caused by first the bullet and then the vehicle crash had left him in a critical condition. Having climbed a slight rise, the little party hid among some rocks while Terry and Andy tried to staunch the flow of blood from Dave's leg wound.

By this time the Iraqis had regrouped and were aiming to surround the three. Andy had left his rifle in the damaged truck, unable to carry both it and the SSM. By firing and moving around Terry kept the Iraqis at bay as his two companions tried desperately to move deeper into the darkness. Dave, now slipping in and out of consciousness, ordered the others to leave while he provided covering fire for them. It was a situation that has arisen many times before, and the choice is never easy. If you stay with a badly wounded man you risk the whole group being captured. And capture by the Iraqis would mean torture and possibly death. On this occasion, even if the Iraqis did not find Dave he would most likely die, but that could take several hours.

While Andy and Terry tried to decide what to do, Dave gave them the order, 'No thanks, Andy. I'll take my chances to the bitter end. Now go.'

As it was highly likely that the SSM would pass out, Andy and Terry decided that the rifle would be more use to the two of them. Paul had managed to grab a 66mm rocket from the damaged vehicle, and this was left with Dave.

With the guys gone, the SSM slipped into unconsciousness once more. It was the sound of voices down in the wadi that snapped him back to reality. Several Iraqi soldiers were standing around a vehicle, and the target was too good to miss. He pulled out the rocket and aimed it at the truck. But just at the moment when he was about to fire, two Iraqi soldiers jumped him.

'Who are you?' they asked in Arabic.

'English,' Dave replied. Although he was a fluent Arabic-speaker, he pretended that he could only speak a few words.

Surprisingly, an officer appeared and a stretcher was called for. Hours later the SSM was being treated by an Iraqi civilian doctor, who did a wonderful job of repairing the injured leg. Eventually Dave was treated in hospital, while his interrogation continued.

One day two interrogators were standing by his bed discussing what question to ask him. But Brian pre-empted them as they turned to speak, which gave away the fact that he spoke fluent Arabic. Despite protests from the medical staff, the two interrogators ripped the drips and other equipment from his body and gave him a real beating. As his condition improved he was paraded around Baghdad with other captured soldiers.

As for Andy and Terry, they made an incredible escape and evaded capture by sheer professionalism. They hid by day and walked by night, and two days later were located by an American A10 tank-buster aircraft. They were then guided to their other half-squadron and finally reached safety.

At the time of the re-supply, Dave was still missing and believed dead. When the war ended, his reappearance delighted his family who had been advised that he was missing in action, possibly dead. The SSM was awarded the Military Cross, a decoration normally given only to commissioned officers.

We also received confirmation that a member of call sign Bravo Two Zero, Chris Ryan, had made it back to Syria and was now sitting back at the air base in Saudi. Nothing else had been heard from any other member of that ill-fated patrol. When the war was over, I sat and talked to Chris at great length over a few beers in Abu Dhabi. Later on I also talked to Andy McNab. There were a few inconsistencies in their stories, but that is only to be expected since they split up soon after they were compromised.

As I understand it, Andy was placed in charge of an eight-man team made up of his own four-man patrol and Vince's. They and two other patrols were to watch the three main motorways coming out of Baghdad. These MSRs not only carried the bulk of the Scuds and military equipment but also linked the six principal bridges which spanned the River Tigris in central Baghdad, all of which were still intact. Apart from connecting the two halves of the city, these bridges carried the landlines which were essential for keeping Baghdad in communication with the rest of the country and with the army in Kuwait. These landlines ran alongside the three MSRs running west-to-east, mainly into Jordan. It would be the patrol's task to find and sabotage these landlines in the northern area. Like the other two Bravo patrols, they would have to operate for fourteen days before receiving any re-supply.

The team spent twelve hours making detailed plans before they were ferried to their drop-off point at last light by a camouflaged Chinook helicopter. The patrol was heavily armed, carrying four M16s all with 203s, while the rest had Minimis machine guns. Each man carried plenty of ammo and a disposable 66mm rocket plus white phosphorus. The weight was enormous, and all of it would have to be carried by the men. Their first attempt to fly into Iraq was aborted, but on 23 January the patrol boarded the helicopter for another try. Their safety depended on the skill of the pilot, and there were anti-aircraft missiles all along the route. Still, as they were going in under the cover of three Coalition air raids there would be little danger of enemy fire.

When the pilot landed at the same refuelling point as on the previous attempt he was given the go-ahead, and the team flew on into Iraq. Then they were spotted by an Iraqi missile crew. The missile locked on and in desperation the Chinook pilot threw his aircraft all over the sky. His efforts were rewarded and the missile was evaded. Half an hour later, the pilot gave a two-minute warning prior to landing. At 2100 hrs the helicopter lifted off and the SAS men were on their own. The whole of the immediate area was desolate, and it was bloody cold. Although Andy had been in the Middle East many times before, this type of terrain was new to him, but the guys were well-armed and very confident. Andy and Vince called them all together. Andy told them where they were, where they were going, and what the rendezvous point would be for the next twenty-four hours. This was just in case there was a crisis and the party got split up. They would go north, aiming for a half-buried petroleum pipeline which should lead to a major ridge line where the RV point was located.

Ferrying their huge amount of equipment they set off. The going was slow, but by 0445 hrs they had reached the bend in the highway. Vince and his men waited while Andy did a recce, looking for a place to hide. After about half an hour he found a perfect site to lie up: a small cave about five metres high, cut into the rock and protected by an overhang which would hide them from view and provide cover from fire.

The team moved all the equipment into the cave, while Andy went out to check the surrounding area. The ground was mostly flat, but about 1500 metres away there was a plantation with a water tower and buildings. According to the map and the OC's briefing, that plantation should not have been there. It was much too close for comfort. Back at the cave they tried to send a report, only to discover that the radio was out of order. This meant returning to the landing site the following night to rendezvous with a helicopter at 0400 and exchange radios.

At first light Andy risked a look over the brim of the wadi. To his surprise, just 300 metres from the cave was a military encampment which his recce patrol the previous night had missed. They prepared to spend the daylight hours sitting in the cave and observing the surrounding area. Although vehicles moved on the nearby MSR, there were no problems until mid-afternoon. A boy herding goats looked over into the wadi, saw the team and promptly bolted to raise the alarm. Andy thought the cave would be useless for defence, and preparations were made to clear out even though it was not yet last night. If forced to fight, they would stand a much better chance in the open.

The team would go west, trying to avoid the Iraqi positions, then head south towards the helicopter RV. They took only their bergens and belt kit, leaving everything else behind. With shamags over their faces so as to look more like the locals, they left in single file.

Just when it seemed that they had got away with it, they heard tracked vehicles on their left-hand side. Knowing that a fight was inevitable, they got down in a defensive position with weapons at the ready. An armoured personnel carrier with a 7.62 machine gun came down the small depression towards them, with another APC bringing up the rear. Both Vince and Legs fired off their 66mm rockets, and a pretty unequal fight ensued. As an Iraqi truck arrived on the scene, a third 66 rocket took it out. But what should they do next? If they remained in a stand-off fight they would soon run out of ammunition. Chris said that at this stage everybody was psyched up and they decided to attack.

Andy, Chris and two guys from Vince's team ran forward while the others provided covering fire; then as they dropped down, the covering party advanced – classic fire and movement towards the enemy. Andy let those with the Minimis get ahead to make use of their superior firepower. When they got to within 50 metres of the APCs, the nearest one pulled back. The guys could hardly believe it; they had driven off an enemy with vastly superior numbers and hardware. The patrol was now on top of the situation, with Iraqi bodies lying everywhere. Still, Andy realised that they would need to get away before reinforcements arrived. Grabbing their bergens they moved off, followed at a distance by a now cautious enemy.

Now that they had been compromised and their mission had become impossible, their one object was to get out. They would soon have the cover of darkness, so they moved quickly. As they ran, two trucks carrying about forty infantry came from the east and started firing. The team retreated up a gradual slope to the west. At the brow of the hill they came under fire from the anti-aircraft guns to the north-west. Things were not looking good, and it was agreed that they should ditch their bergens in order to move faster. The enemy finally lost contact as darkness fell, and the team melted away.

At a rallying point Andy stopped and counted the heads, pleased that they were still together. Although the radio was gone they still had four TACBEs – tactical reconnaissance beacons – and decided to use one. There was no reply, and no chance of contact unless a jet flew overhead, when they would call on the emergency frequency.

Andy decided to head for Syria, 120 kilometres to the west. The enemy would expect them to head south towards Saudi, so they figured they might make it by moving south and boxing to the north-west. The main problem was the combination of cold and all the running they had been doing. Their shirts were wet with sweat and the cold ripped at the damp cloth. A check with Magellan showed that they had travelled 25 kilometres from the cave; it was time to start boxing, and cross the MSR before first light.

They travelled on a compass bearing, stopping for five minutes every hour to drink and rest as some of the guys were close to exhaustion. The night became very black, and the temperature dropped even further. After another 15 kilometres, they turned north. Around this time Andy noticed that they had slowed down, and that there were gaps in the line. Vince had injured his leg during the escape, and Stan was dangerously dehydrated. Chris, the medic, helped a little by putting two sachets of electrolyte into Stan's water bottle.

Andy now changed the order of the march, putting Chris as lead scout, with Stan and Vince behind him, followed by Andy and the rest of the patrol. They moved off once more, but Chris said the pace got even slower. Both Vince's and Stan's condition declined, and everyone was feeling the effects of the cold and the night's marching.

Once, hearing an aircraft approaching from the north, Andy risked trying the TACBE again. They gathered around as an American voice answered, albeit somewhat garbled. The signal was weakening as the jet flew out of range, but the pilot had repeated their call sign and this gave them hope.

They staggered off once more. Those who were slow opened up the group which caused the patrol to become split. Chris, Stan and Vince, who had been at the front, were suddenly missing. Andy's group waited a while, afraid to shout or show a light because there might have been enemy around. When no one appeared, they could only hope that they would eventually rendezvous. They moved on, and two hours later Andy's party crossed the MSR.

When daylight came, they found a small knoll topped by a cairn surrounded by a low wall. By building this up slightly, they formed a reasonable shelter. As they huddled together, Andy got out his map and did some calculations. He reckoned that in the last twelve hours, running for their lives, they had travelled some 85 kilometres.

With the dawn came icy cold rain, and they huddled together to share their body warmth. All code sheets were burnt, and everyone checked their pockets for compromising material. They heard vehicle sounds in the distance and spotted two APCs about one kilometre to the south, but they caused no problems. The rain turned to snow. The exhausted men in their soaking clothes were now exposed to freezing wind. Andy scraped a small hole and lit a hexy block to brew up a hot drink; it made the difference between life and death.

Stan, Vince and Chris were having just as hard a time. After losing contact with the others they had pushed on, and by daybreak had found themselves out in the open. The only cover they could find was a deep tank track where the three of them lay throughout the day, battered by the wind and covered with snow. As the darkness fell they could hardly move – the cold had stiffened their muscles and eaten into their bones. That night as they moved off, Vince was in desperate trouble. Time after time he staggered and fell, and at last he simply wandered away. When they realised that he was missing Stan and Chris searched for over an hour, but there was no sign of him.

Andy knew that it was becoming just a matter of survival for all of them. Mark was in a very bad way, so Andy and Simon huddled round him and gave him their body heat while Fred and Legs prepared some hot food. The danger of death from hypothermia was now greater than that of being captured. After two hours they got going again, struggling on through the darkness.

At midnight the patrol realised that they were following a dried-up river bed, which was a little sheltered and warmer. But a near miss with two Iraqis forced them to climb up again. By the early hours it was obvious that Mark was on the verge of collapse, so they returned to the river bed and found a depression in the ground where they huddled together for warmth. They would try again tomorrow. By dawn the weather had changed to clear skies and sunshine, though it was still bitterly cold. The outlook seemed better, although they were short of water, and they reckoned that another twelve hours' hard march that night would see them at the border.

The same sunshine had given Stan and Chris a new lease of life. They had fallen exhausted into a small dried up river bed, and were now sitting against one wall. As the sun warmed them, they sorted out their equipment and cleaned their weapons. About midday they spotted a young goatherd out with his flock. The boy was friendly, and Stan had gone off with him – though against Chris's advice – to investigate the possibility of acquiring a vehicle. Chris waited until it was dark, by which time Stan had not returned. Fearful that his companion might have been captured, he started walking. He was now on his own.

Strangely enough, later that day Andy's group too encountered a goatherd with his flock. He was a friendly character in his seventies who seemed to think that they were connected with the Iraqi army. They all sat down together to share food and conversation. Everyone enjoyed his goats' milk, and he went on his way unharmed. However, as a precaution the team headed south for a while before turning west once more.

With only two days' food left and almost out of water, they decided to hijack a vehicle. The plan was to creep down to the road, where Simon would pretend he was a cripple and Andy would support him. The others would hide, ready to pounce when some good Samaritan stopped. It took half an hour to reach the road; twenty minutes later a vehicle approached, slowing down when Simon and Andy appeared in its headlights. It was, of all things, a 1950s New York yellow cab, tarted up with typical Arab decoration. The passengers in the back were both soldiers, father and son. They and the driver were quickly tied up and abandoned unharmed in a ditch.

Andy drove off, with Legs beside him giving directions with a compass. The taxi had half a tank of fuel, which, all being well, was enough to get them over the border by morning. They planned to drive as far as possible, dump the vehicle and then cross on foot. Their map, being an air chart, was not very helpful and the roads were very confusing. Presently, as they moved through villages and countryside, they came to a slow-moving traffic jam. Iraqi soldiers were checking all vehicles and eventually they were discovered. Legs shot one man with his rifle, while the others opened up with their Minimis and killed two more squaddies.

At this point they were forced to abandon the taxi and go on foot. Once they were clear of the checkpoint, the fire died down. Andy did a quick check and found that none of the team had been hit. He quickly checked the Magellan; they were about 13 kilometres from the border and had nine hours of darkness left. They travelled close to another road with a heavily built-up area to their left, taking cover every time a car passed.

At last, coming over a crest, they looked down on the lights of Abu Kamal and Krabilah, the two built-up areas that straddled the border. There was a lot of noise coming from the nearest town as Coalition jets carried out an air raid. The team walked on, using the confusion to cover their escape.

They were now almost at the Euphrates and took cover at the edge of a plantation. Mark used the Magellan; it was still 10 kilometres to the border. They travelled slowly, stopping every five minutes, checking buildings before skirting them. Now it was just seven kilometres to go. But their luck did not hold: they were seen, and in the ensuing exchange of fire Mark and Andy got separated from the others.

They were on the river ban, some 10–15 metres above the water, hiding among the bushes on the first of a series of small plateaus that lay between them and some ploughed land that they had crossed. The Iraqis were on the opposite bank, hunting for them with torches. Tracers and bullets were still flying. It was impossible to cross the river, which was icy and in full flow. The only way out was through the enemy positions.

Following the ploughed field, parallel to the river, the two men crawled along the muddy furrows for twenty minutes. Suddenly they were challenged. Mark fired and shot one soldier, and then both were running once more. The enemy seemed to think that a full-scale invasion was in progress, and in the confusion Andy hoped they might slip through unnoticed. They had two and a half hours of darkness left in which to reach the border.

THE COST OF WAR

They came to a three-strand barbed wire fence which they would have to cross; it led to an Iraqi truck compound. They cleared the fence between two canvas-topped trucks, but as Mark went over the wire twanged. A soldier in one of the trucks heard and started jabbering. Andy shot him and, going up to his truck, raked it with fire before lobbing a grenade into the other. Now both men were out of ammo. Dropping their weapons, they bolted.

Just before first light, as they ploughed through the muck of a large rubbish dump, two AK assault rifles opened up at close range. Both men instinctively dropped down, but Mark didn't get up again.

Andy ran on alone, but he felt that the worst was over – just a quick dash to the border and he would be free. His feet were now soaking wet, and icy cold, and his boots were caked with heavy mud. He also had deep cuts on his hands, knees and elbows, bruising on the sides of both legs, and scratches and gashes from thorns and wire; but worse was soon to follow. Andy stopped to weigh up the situation. Navigation was easy, as the mast on the Iraqi side of the border was visible ahead. He could still hear firing coming from behind him, and on balance it seemed best to lie up and wait one more night. He was very hungry and devoured his last sachet of food, washing it down by sucking up a little water from the ditch in which he had concealed himself. He then lay back and waited.

The morning was bright and cold when Andy was awakened a while later to the sound of gunfire coming from a nearby steel bridge. Then a soldier who was searching under the bridge saw him. Seconds later a number of men jumped into the ditch and hauled him out by his feet. A savage beating with feet and fists followed. He was hit and kicked about his body and head, but somehow remained conscious. Then, forcing Andy to his knees, they tied his hands and hauled him to a vehicle. As the soldiers passed through a town they fired their AK47s into the air, and the vehicle was soon surrounded by a howling mob. They swarmed all over the vehicle to get at the prisoner, spitting, slapping, punching and kicking. A lynching seemed to be on the cards, but at last the soldiers drove the crowd away.

Eventually Andy was taken to a barracks where he was dragged from the vehicle and thrown to the ground. The first thing he saw was another body lying with hands and feet tied together. It was covered in blood and dirt and the head was horribly swollen, but he recognised it as Fred. At least one other member of the patrol was alive. A continuous round of beatings and interrogations ensued. Both Andy and Fred took everything the Iraqis could give them; painful though it was, they survived.

After a while it became obvious that the interrogations were not for any specific purpose and that the brutality was just for fun. After being moved to several different locations the pair finally found themselves being driven to Baghdad. When the vehicle stopped, they were dragged across a cobbled courtyard. This was agony to Andy's injured feet, as his wounds broke open and began to bleed again. They were made to sit cross-legged on the floor of a semi-dark room with damp stone walls. Their blindfolds were ripped off and for the first time Andy saw Fred close enough to make eye contact. Talking was not allowed, but it was necessary; eye contact alone said a thousand words and bolstered their morale.

The interrogations did not become violent but continued for a long time. Andy stuck to his cover story and acted broken and pathetic. Soon he was put in the same cell as Fred, where they shared a blanket and Andy learned what had happened to his patrol. Fred, Legs and Simon had been involved in a fire-fight after the group had split up. Simon had been shot, so only Legs and Fred had made it to the river. They had searched for boats but, finding none, had to resort to swimming. The water had been bitterly cold, which had almost finished Legs off.

Fred had dragged him out of the water to a small pump-hut, where he had lain exhausted. By morning Fred could see that Legs would die without medical attention, so he had beckoned a nearby farmer. Leaving Legs, who was still dozing, to a better fate, Fred had slipped away. However, the locals had spotted Fred and pounced, using his shamag to tie his hands. When Fred had last seen Legs, he was on a stretcher and appeared to be dead.

Some days later, as Andy was looking past the guards into the corridor, he saw Stan being dragged past. He was in a dreadful state, covered in blood and apparently lifeless. But when Andy saw Stan for a second time, albeit in a bad way, at least he was still alive.

On the afternoon of 6 February Andy was blindfolded, handcuffed and put into the back of a vehicle. The English-speaking guards in front teased and chatted. They said that they could see Fred and Stan in the car ahead. Andy was taken to the military prison and led to a cell, with a blanket over his head. Presently someone came and asked if he would like to be with his friends, and at last the three were reunited in another cell.

Once more they compared notes and speculated that all the others were probably dead. Stan was fairly sure that Vince must have died of exposure – he had been in a pretty bad way the evening they had lost him. Then they had met the goatherd and Stan had gone off with him to look for a vehicle. When they got to the herdsman's hut there were two vehicles outside. Stan watched the place for about twenty minutes, planning to take one of them if the keys had been left in the ignition. But as he approached the vehicles, an Iraqi soldier came out of the house. He tried to pull a weapon out of the nearest vehicle, but Stan shot him. Several Iraqi squaddies then rushed out of the house. Stan shot three, then his gun jammed. He tried to get away in one of the vehicles but the five remaining soldiers attacked him with rifle butts, knocking him down. Once they had tied him up they took him to a military installation near the Euphrates. His interrogation followed the usual pattern.

One night an injured American Marine pilot was dragged in and gave them the news that the ground war was nearly over. On the morning of 3 March, Stan and Fred were told they were going home, but it appeared that Andy was being kept back as a hostage. Then on 15 March all the remaining prisoners in the block, including Andy, were told that they were going home too.

After Stan's disappearance Chris had been without water for two days and so made his way down to the river, where he sank in deep mud to his waist. He then lay up in a small wadi until nightfall, moving off again as darkness fell. After staggering around in this way for several days, Chris came upon an illuminated road sign. He found he was still 50 kilometres from the border, and had badly estimated his position. With his water gone he was dehydrating fast, but as luck would have it he found a stream. Although he had septic cuts on his hands and his feet were in an appalling condition, Chris struggled forward until he eventually crossed into Syria. A few days later he was reunited with the squadron in Saudi Arabia. And that is the story of Bravo Two Zero.

I must admit that Chris was quite pissed when he told me his version, and having read both Andy's and Chris's books I say this. No one can take away from them or the other members of the patrol what they did. They took the right decisions and in the end they took the beatings. Bravo One Zero and Bravo Two Zero, both of whom had a vehicle to move their equipment, decided that they were not going to stop in Iraq. One patrol just got back on the chopper and flew back to Saudi, while the other realised that the operation was not viable and drove out within a few days. They were both given a real hard time.

As for us, once the re-supply was over we were ordered once

more to go chasing Scuds. On one occasion I topped a small rise and observed some Iraqi movement way out to our front. Looking through the scope, I observed a very large concentration of Iraqi military. I could clearly see the antennas and the vehicles moving around. I withdrew behind cover. When Brian arrived and enquired, 'What the fuck was happening' – his usual greeting – I told him of the enemy sighting. And so of course he drove his vehicle to the top of the small rise and stood on the cab with a set of binoculars. Seconds later he turned around, mouthing his second favourite phrase: 'Fucking Bedu'.

Later that evening Brian called us all together and issued the following decree: 'The next time some jumped up little corporal starts questioning my orders, he'll be out on the next available chopper. Now keep your fucking suggestions to yourselves in future.' With this, he and his shadow Mel went off together.

Men like Brian are quite unusual in the SAS, but just now and again one slips through the net. Back in Hereford you can just avoid them – give them enough rope and they will hang themselves. But quite apart from the petty bickering, most of which can be put down to nervous tension, feelings in our column had been running very high up to the Victor Two operation.

When it became obvious that Brian had lost his rifle he got a right old slagging. At first he kept it a secret, but we found out. Then he started demanding that one of the guys give him their weapon. The older ones told him to fuck off, so he picked on a junior member of the team.

Brian is now a quartermaster with the TA, and holds the Queen's commission with the rank of major. For his actions throughout the Gulf operation he was awarded the Distinguished Conduct Medal, one of the highest awards given by the British army. After the war, Mel received a mention in despatches for his part in the operation. None of us knew what he got it for, but he was recommended by Brian. I always thought of Mel as Muttley, Dick Dastardly's dog: 'Me. Me. Me.'

As the ground war to rescue Kuwait got under way we were ordered to move south, but not to cross back into Saudi Arabia. This we did, waiting until the Coalition ground forces had re-taken the city. Then, twenty-four hours before the ground war finished, we crossed the border back into Saudi Arabia. All the guys were very happy to be back in a friendly country. It was as if some giant blanket had been lifted, and the relief showed on everyone's face. Brian wanted to take a photograph of all the group but Pat, Slugger and I stayed at the back out of view – we were not in the mood.

We had been lucky; some of the other SAS units had suffered badly. I was grateful just to be alive, knowing that I would go home and see my boys again. Maybe my nightly prayer had been heard after all.

I am proud of the part the SAS played in the Gulf War. We did well, operating in very difficult conditions. Many of the guys were tested to the very limit, and came out the better for it. Some, like my friend Shug – Lance Corporal David Denbury, had given their lives. This young man was my patrol signaller and an instantly likeable person. We admired him for his professionalism, but it was his sense of humour and joke telling for which he will be remembered.

As a result of forty-five days behind Iraqi lines the squadron received a DSM, two MCs, 4 MMs and four MIDs. Two were killed and one was captured. Then we received official thanks from the Coalition commander, General Norman Schwarz-kopf. Storming Norman came to see us one day, and we all lined up to shake his hand. He told us he was proud of us and how well we had done. Just a few days after the war was over a letter of commendation arrived.

* * *

THE COST OF WAR

Letter of Commendation for
the 22nd Special Air Service SAS Regiment

1. I wish to officially commend the 22nd Special Air Service SAS Regiment for their totally outstanding performance of military operations during Operation Desert Storm.

2. Shortly after the initiation of a strategic air campaign, it became apparent that the Coalition forces would be unable to eliminate Iraq's firing of Scud missiles from western Iraq into Israel. The continued firing of Scuds on Israel carried with it enormous unfavourable ramifications and could have resulted in the dismantling of the carefully crafted Coalition. Such a dismantling would have adversely affected in ways difficult to measure the ultimate outcome of the military campaign. It became apparent that the only way that the Coalition could succeed in reducing these Scud launches was by physically placing military forces on the ground in the vicinity of the western launch sites. At that time, the majority of available Coalition forces were committed to the forthcoming military campaign in the eastern portion of the theatre of operations.

Further, none of these forces possessed the requisite skills and abilities required to conduct such a dangerous operation. The only force deemed qualified for this critical mission was the 22nd Special Air Service SAS Regiment.

3. From the first day they were assigned their mission until the last day of conflict, the performance of the 22nd Special Air Service SAS Regiment was courageous and highly professional. The area in which they were committed proved to contain far more numerous enemy forces than had been predicted by every intelligence estimate, the terrain was much more difficult than expected and the weather conditions were unseasonably brutal. Despite these hazards, in a very short period of time the 22nd Special Air Service SAS Regiment was successful in totally denying the central corridor of western Iraq to Iraqi Scud units. The result was that the principal areas used by the Iraqis to fire Scuds on Tel Aviv were no longer available to them. They were required to move their Scud missile firing forces to the

north-west portion of Iraq and from that location the firing of Scud missiles was essentially militarily ineffective.

4. While it became necessary to introduce United States Special Operations Forces into the area to attempt to close down the north-west Scud areas, the 22nd Special Air Service SAS Regiment provided invaluable assistance to the US forces. They took every possible measure to ensure that US forces were thoroughly briefed and were able to profit from the valuable lessons that had been learned by earlier SAS deployments into western Iraq.

I am completely convinced that had US forces not received these thorough indoctrinations by SAS personnel, US forces would have suffered a much higher rate of casualties than was ultimately the case. Further, the SAS and US joint forces immediately merged into a combined fighting force where the synergetic effect of these fine units ultimately caused the enemy to be convinced that they were facing forces in western Iraq that were more than tenfold the size of those they were actually facing. As a result, large numbers of enemy forces that might otherwise have been deployed in the eastern theatre were tied down in western Iraq.

5. The performance of the 22nd Special Air Service SAS Regiment during Operation Desert Storm was in the highest traditions of the professional military service and in keeping with the proud history and tradition that has been established by that regiment. Please ensure that this commendation receives appropriate attention and is passed on to the unit and its members.

> H. NORMAN SCHWARZKOPF
> General, US Army
> Commander in Chief

7

FIGHTING ON THE HOME FRONT

oming home should have been a plus in itself, and in some ways I consider myself lucky. But we did not return home to a heroes' welcome; as with all SAS operations, when it was over we just disappeared and left the praise for generals and politicians. In the main, the guys are just glad to be with their loved ones – within six months the Gulf War would be nothing more than a fading memory. But for me things got worse rather than better.

The boys had started telling me that they were not happy living with their mother. One evening around our dinner table the boys told Tara and me things that upset us a great deal. Eventually Tara butted in while Matthew was talking, 'They can't stay there any longer. They've got to come and live with us.'

I was devastated. Partly I was angry with myself because I had known for a couple of months that matters were deteriorating. On a few occasions I had taken it upon myself to investigate how June was looking after the boys. I was particularly concerned about them sometimes being left alone at night.

Despite the difficulties, Tara and I knew what we had to do. The boys were very pleased when I explained what we proposed. Next morning after breakfast I put them on the school transport and then began the task of gaining custody. I phoned my solicitor first, asking for an interview that morning, then Tara and I went along to the Social Services at the local council. To our amazement, there was already a case file. They had been made aware of the situation by Matthew's school, which was worried about his health and well-being. They told us that they would give us full backing. The SAS families officer was in total agreement and informed the commanding officer. The people in Social Services said they would tell June when she returned.

There followed an extraordinary sequence of events as June fought me every inch of the way for custody of he boys. Damien and Matthew were eventually interviewed by a judge in chambers to determine which parent they would be happier living with, but even then June was still arguing. I was told that the judge became very angry and told her legal advisers to get their client in order.

The boys coped well with this trauma in their lives. When I was sent overseas Tara was left to cope with them on her own. She did a wonderful job, especially given her problems with the fire brigade.

When the day of the final hearing arrived we all went to court. June conceded overall custody to me, but demanded reasonable access. She had decided to return to Yorkshire to live near her family, and wanted me to bring them to her for visits. This was just not ideal from the children's point of view, so we refused. We wanted her to see them at least once a month for the next six months. Then, if everything went all right on those visits, she could have them to stay at her house in Yorkshire provided it was suitable for Matthew. With my private life improving it was time to get back to some soldiering, although new pressures were arising from Tara.

In December 1993 Tara left the fire brigade because of poor health. She had started suffering badly with her nerves and it became increasingly difficult to communicate with her. A little later it was confirmed that there would be an industrial tribunal at which Tara would be up against the fire brigade and county council to complain about the way she had been treated. A psychologist diagnosed her as suffering from clinical depression, and it was decided that she would be given a medical discharge. From this point onwards our already failing marriage started to disintegrate.

I was now with the Northern Ireland wing instructing students for covert operations and working an average of sixteen hours a day, much of it at night. Because I was to take over the running of the department I had to put in a lot of work to show my bosses that I was capable of doing the job. While serving in Northern Ireland the year before, I had been unfaithful to Tara. She had found out about it and we separated for a couple of weeks, but after numerous phone calls we decided to try again. Unfortunately it was never to be the same again.

Tara had to face some very hard questioning at the tribunal – they threw everything at her in an attempt to make her out to be a liar. Firstly they tried to suggest that my affair in Northern Ireland was the cause of Tara's breakdown, though eventually this was disproved by a psychologist. But what really got to me was when I discovered that, although Tara had told a colleague in confidence about Matthew, he had told every man on her watch.

During the tribunal the attention from TV and newspaper reporters was outrageous but I was granted a media block mainly because of my security status. From that point on the press and TV people were great. Tara did two stories, one on television with BBC Midlands and the other with one of the tabloids. The newspaper reporter told me that Tara's story would be worth a lot of money; Tara and I agreed to donate it to charity. So when the story came out the newspaper gave a cheque to the local Hereford Muscular Dystrophy Group.

In the end a combination of these people and pressures

wrecked a young woman's career, ruined her health and helped sabotage our marriage. I didn't help matters when I had a second affair. Tara left believing that I was still having an affair, which I wasn't. I hold the fire brigade responsible for the loss of all that. To this day I think she was a wonderful woman who, despite Matthew's illness, did everything possible to build a family.

It was very difficult trying to handle so many problems all at once. June was pestering me for money, Tara had the fire brigade, Matthew was not getting any better and the SAS didn't seem to care. I could not sleep, and while I lay I tried to work some way out – but nothing presented itself. Then I started to get strange dreams. I was back in the Gulf, back at Victor Two, and I was repeatedly killing the young Iraqi soldier. This scenario would play over and over again in my mind like a loop of tape. Yet it was not really the Iraqi whom I was seeing, but Matthew.

It was around this time that Yvonne came into my life. She was a military secretary working for the SAS and at first we simply built up a great friendship and genuine affection for each other. When my marriage to Tara started to collapse, I started to confide in Yvonne more and more. A relationship was inevitable. Four months into our affair and Tara found out, which was the catalyst for her eventual departure.

The help and support that Yvonne showed me over an incredibly difficult period were fantastic. Coping with Matthew, trying to make a life away from the SAS, and my recurrent nightmares: amid all this she was my anchor. As Matthew declines, I shall need her more and more.

On 7 December 1995, one of the worst fears of my life was realised when Matthew was taken into hospital. He has been admitted many times during his short life, but eventually the inevitable day came when his disease became too much for him and us to handle. The previous day I had received a call from Matthew's school, Derway College. The doctor there thought it best Matthew should be admitted to the Royal Shrewsbury Hospital.

For some inexplicable reason I drove slowly, arriving around 2 p.m. The sight of him lying there filled me with anger because there's nothing I can do to help him. I can do most things, but this is beyond me.

I left the hospital at 11 p.m. and drove back to Hereford feeling emotionally drained. At times like this some people need others around them but I just wanted to be alone – and to spend as much time with my son as possible. Over the years, while serving abroad with the SAS, I have missed so many things that I would like to have shared with him. Alone in my bed, the tears ran down my cheeks.

The ringing of the telephone woke me; it was a call from the hospital to say that they were moving Matthew down to intensive care because it was becoming difficult for him to breathe. I leaped out of bed and within minutes I was heading back to Shrewsbury. A terrible sight greeted me. My son lay on the bed, a small bundle beneath starched white sheets. Tubes and wires were plugged into various parts of his body. Heads turned as I stood there. 'I'm his father,' I said, addressing no one in particular.

A man moved away from the bed and introduced himself as Charlie, the head doctor. He led me out into the corridor and explained the situation clearly and calmly. He came across as a decisive man, and he remained positive about Matthew's condition. I had to wait about an hour before they allowed me to see my son, but from then on, I could come and go as I wished.

Matthew still required physio throughout the day in order to draw off the liquid that was gathering on his chest. During this time he was very heavily sedated and a ventilator helped him to breathe. Occasionally he would wake up and look around. He recognised me immediately and I detected a slight change to his facial muscles – he was pleased to see me.

Charlie had said that, no matter how much or for how long you prepare yourself for such a day, the sight still hits hard. He was right. The minute you see your loved one surrounded by all those people and machines, with tubes protruding from their nose and wires and tubes in their arms, monitors for heart rate, oxygen saturation and blood pressure all ticking or humming in front of you, it just kills you. You put on a brave face, but inside you are falling apart. I looked into Matthew's eyes, knowing that he knows, even though I've never told him. He's going to die. With false bravado, I asked him if he felt okay. He shook his head.

'Do you feel like shit, son?'

He nodded.

'I love you, son.'

He nodded and tried to speak, but the words would not come.

'I love you – do you love me, son?' I asked, anticipating his words.

He looked me squarely in the eyes and nodded, and then I let him rest. I have resigned myself to the fact that I am going to lose Matthew, whom I love beyond belief. But at times my guilt does get the better of me. My guilty feelings arise because of my infidelity. It's not because of the act itself, which to me doesn't matter in the slightest – in truth I've always been here for my two sons, Matthew in particular – but because I have stripped them of a mother. I am guilty also of taking life. More and more the face of that young Iraqi haunts my sleep: I see his body, but Matthew's face. I feel as if I am paying penance for a crime. Losing one of my sons is the hardest thing I shall ever have to go through – just sitting and watching him slip from the world.

At 10 p.m. the nursing staff changed over and Matthew had to be given some physiotherapy. Most of them were brilliant, but that night, just when I least needed it, I got a patronising one who just told me to leave. Couldn't she at least have introduced herself? Asked me politely if I could leave for a little while and explained why? 'Piss off, I've got a job to do and you're in the way,' was her attitude. Heaven knows, what I was going through was distressing enough without being treated like a piece of shit. I had lived with Matthew and his illness for seventeen years, and had lost count of the times I had given him physio myself.

So, not surprisingly in the circumstances, I lost my temper and used words I normally reserve for SAS recruits, then stormed off. She followed and tried to apologise, but I couldn't cope and just told her to fuck off. I realised deep down that she was just doing her best for my son, and the sudden tension and anger sent me into the toilets for a good cry. Eventually I got a grip of myself and phoned Yvonne; just hearing her voice made me feel better.

Back at the ward they were worried about Matthew's breathing and decided to put him on 100 per cent oxygen which would allow him to relax and even get some sleep. Then I went home to collect some clothes and other items because they had offered me a small room in the hospital where I could sleep. Despite all the wires and tubes Matthew managed to raise a smile, trying to tell us that he wanted to say sorry.

I said, 'Sorry mate, I haven't got a clue what you're on about.' It cheered me to see that his sense of humour had not got lost. My boy was still hanging in there.

At 2 a.m. when I returned Charlie told me they had had to catheter Matthew because he was unable to go to the toilet. They had also wanted to put a line down his nose into his stomach, but this had distressed Matthew so much that they

had decided against it. As soon as I walked into the ward
Matthew awoke. It was as though, despite being heavily
sedated, he knew I was there. I leaned over and kissed him
on the forehead, as I always have done to both my boys since
they were very small.

'Goodnight and God bless. See you in the morning. Love you,
mate.' This little ritual would normally be repeated by both my
sons, but that night Matthew could not answer.

Next day it was clear that Matthew would indeed have to
have a tube fitted down into his stomach. A little later he
complained of pains in his chest and the vital signs monitor
started to bleep. One of the nurses came running and quickly
realised that one of his ventilator pipes was full of water. After
she had emptied it Matthew instantly felt better. Warm water is
filtered into the system to allow moisture into his chest to break
up the mucus, and this in turn allows the chest to be drained
easier.

In the afternoon, while Matthew rested, I went to collect
Damien from his school in nearby Oswestry. This was the
moment I had been dreading: explaining to him the full
reality of Matthew's condition. I had to tell him that his
brother's illness was terminal: at best we could expect him to
last for another five years, but on the other hand we could
lose him today. When this happened, we would have to
support each other as best we could. Damien took the news
badly and we were both very upset. I told him that Matthew
must know nothing of this; in the end Damien assured me
that he would be strong, and added that he wanted to stay at
the hospital with me. At 10.30 I sent him to bed because he
looked so tired. He said goodnight to Matthew and walked
off to the small room. About an hour later I put my head
around the door to see Damien sleeping peacefully. He is a
wonderful son who gives me more support than he realises,
and I love him dearly.

A couple of days later I had a bad telephone conversation with Yvonne. I knew she was trying to help me, but I found it upsetting listening to somebody talking about getting ready for Christmas. What do I care about decorating the tree and wrapping presents? Damien and I will be here in hospital with Matthew.

Earlier I had spoken to Nana on the phone – it was her ninetieth birthday. She had had a good day at the races and was celebrating with the family. It made me feel a little down to hear all the voices in the background laughing and enjoying themselves.

My constant main concern was Matthew, who was finding it very difficult to breathe even if there was just a small amount of water in the ventilator pipes. For the first time he had asked me to hold his hand. This in itself worried me, because he very rarely showed his emotions. But I had actually been feeling quite tired and ill myself. I was bothered about Damien. I was worried about Yvonne. I was afraid the SAS would think I was having too much time off. I fretted about the future. But most of all I was fucking terrified that I was going to lose my son. Would I be able to cope with the pressure? All I could think was: God give me strength.

Matthew had a poor night, producing lots of saliva which had to be drained off with the suction pipe all the time. There was pneumonia in his right lung and pain in the left. He was also upset by the death of a trauma patient who had been admitted late last night and kept in the same ward. After his death the patient's family arrived, and I think Matthew envisaged his own death.

I started to notice differences between the shifts of nursing staff. Most were good but some were poor. One crew ignored the fact that Matthew had soiled himself. I was not impressed by a nurse saying that because he was not really lying in it they would clean it up in two hours' time. As a result I was horrible

171

to Yvonne on the phone, then phoned back to apologise which made both of us feel better.

For most of the night I lay awake and thought about Matthew. People don't really understand what it's like to be permanently in a wheelchair. Graham, a friend who looked after Matthew when I was away, told me he and his mates once took him to the night club in Hereford. The wheelchair had caused some problems, especially getting it into the toilet. So these four big bearded rocker types, all dressed in leather waistcoats lifted Matthew's wheelchair in and held it there for him. Anybody who got in the way was manhandled out until he had finished. Later some dickheads decided to use Matthew's tray, which is attached to his chair, as a table on which to rest their pints. Graham got annoyed – which, considering his size, was not good for them – and had to be restrained by his mates from killing the offenders.

Down in the ward Matthew's pulse rate suddenly started climbing dramatically and he couldn't breathe properly. The nurse and I managed to get him to relax before I kissed him goodnight. Simon, the charge nurse, offered me a cup of tea and I found myself pouring out all my grievances to him. None of the doctors had spoken to me apart from Charlie on the first day. Nobody had bothered to let me know what was going on. It was stressing me out badly, and I wanted something done about it. Simon made all the right sounds and nodded his head. I knew that blasting him out would do no good, but at least I had got it off my chest.

Come Monday morning I realised that my message of displeasure had been passed on to the consultant. Suddenly everyone started being very nice. All the doctors, including the consultant, explained what they were doing, while all the other staff smiled.

The doctors had decided to remove Matthew's tube and perform a mini-tracheotomy. This meant inserting a small sealable valve into his throat which would allow a tube to be inserted direct into his windpipe and down into his lungs, enabling them to be drained. The operation was successfully completed in the afternoon, and Matthew fell asleep. For several hours in the morning the nurses had tried to get a needle into the blood vessels in his wrist or feet, which would allow them to position a microchip sensor and connect it to a monitor. But they failed because Matthew's blood vessels are so small and hard to locate. What with that and the mini-trach, he was totally exhausted.

A couple of days later Matthew had improved enough to be transported back to Hereford by ambulance. My fears were fewer, but I was still not convinced that he would make it. I talked to the doctor that day and explained my personal problems and situation. He levelled with me and said he thought that Damien and I should have some sort of counselling. He also felt that Matthew should talk to someone, and I agreed. Although it was hard to think that he would be told the full extent of his illness, I was beginning to believe it would be the best thing. The doctor explained to me that when the time came either Matthew's heart would just stop and he would lose consciousness and slip away, or he would find it no longer possible to breathe. Either way, he assured me, it would be painless and at last his suffering would be over.

8

WAITING FOR MY FUTURE

I had decided to leave the SAS. This might not have been a wise decision, but I was too stressed out to contemplate anything else. In an ordinary regiment things would have been different but in the SAS there is no room for anyone with long-term family problems. I had no other choice: it was the SAS or Matthew. How could I possibly go off for several months knowing that he might die at any time? What kind of father would I be? What kind of human being would I be? About a week before I was due to leave the army, I went into camp to see the doc. I told him about being unable to cope, and about the nightmares I was having, and he arranged for me to see a specialist.

The psychiatrist, who was working in Northern Ireland, made an appointment and on the day in question the army flew her over in a helicopter. She was very good, and soon I was sitting there pouring my heart out to her. The tears had been there for a long time, and although I hate myself for being weak, crying helps to relieve the tension. I started at the beginning, which was around the time of the Gulf War, and stopped when I got to Matthew.

'You realise that you are ill,' she said with some concern.

'What do you mean? Am I going off my head?' It would not have come as any great surprise.

'Your problem is PTSD – post traumatic stress disorder. You've been under stress for so long that your mind is fighting to control your fragmenting thoughts. First you had the tension associated with fighting behind the lines in the Gulf. Then you

177

returned to a potential divorce and serious problems with Tara. Now you're trying to provide a life for Matthew and Damien. The ups and downs in Matthew's health are keeping you at the same stress level as you had during the Gulf War. At some stage you'll have to come down, or to be honest you'll go mad. I'm surprised you haven't cracked long ago.'

Tell me something I don't know! I thought. But what do I do about it? It is difficult for me to make plans, mainly because I have to devote much of my time to caring for the boys, especially Matthew. It greatly restricts what I can do, bearing in mind that most of the work offered to ex-SAS men involves security, close protection and similar scenarios. Unfortunately these jobs are situated in the world's trouble spots and take you away from home for long periods.

But then again, just making ends meet demands that I take on work, although I try for jobs with short contracts – a month at most. Even then I am constantly haunted by the thought of not being there when Matthew takes a turn for the worse. Whenever I am away, I have three men to stay with Matthew who look after his every need. Normally they do a three days on, six days off roster, and without them I simply could not manage.

When I was about to leave the army, a friend of mine, Tony, asked if I would be interested in looking after a Middle-Eastern Minister. The job was mostly London-based and I would be kept on a retainer plus a very good salary. I needed work, I had bills to pay and we had to eat. Tony got me the job.

But really I want to be an actor! This idea started to form in my mind when Tony was asked to provide a couple of guys who would be willing to enact an aircraft hijack for an ITN documentary about another ex-SAS guy, Barry Davies. Seventeen years ago he had shot a Palestinian terrorist, and now he was trying to save her life. Tony and I met Barry and I drove the three of us to Southend airport, where we would be using a Boeing 727 kindly loaned by some Arab sheikh. Barry had written several books since leaving the regiment and was about to publish one on escape, evasion and survival. Later a film company wanted to make a video of the book and Barry asked me if I would be interested in the starring role. Of course I would!

We made the film in Jersey, and it was great fun. I was part of a four-man SAS patrol working in Bosnia on a laser target marking operation. During a fire-fight, two of the guys get killed. A third is shot badly in the leg and as a result we are both captured, but I escape. And what an escape; knocking out guards, jumping fences, being chased by dogs and eating rabbits. Then came the blow: Tony rang to say that I had been sacked from my bodyguard job. That was my main income down the drain, and I had just taken out a mortgage on a new house.

I was distraught, but Barry kept me going and his own track record was a great encouragement. A few years back his wife had left him with two kids and no money. What did he do? He went out and built a house with his own hands, then he sat down and started to write books which are doing very well.

He was right: a new job in Oman came up for me straight-away. The moment this finished another film job came up, with the promise of yet more to follow.

Now all I have to do is wait – wait for Matthew to leave me. I know in my heart that when that time comes it will hurt, and I steel myself. Each day we look at each other and laugh over some little joke, and I wonder how our lives would have turned out if things had been different. I am six foot six and fairly well-built, and there is Matthew so small and hunched up. Yet what you see is only the physical appearance; inside, he is far stronger than me. If there is a God, take care of my boy, and at the moment of his parting spare a thought for me.